A Vision of Unity

The History of the Bakery and Confectionery Workers International Union

by

Stuart Bruce Kaufman

Distributed by the
University of Illinois Press

8

Distributed by the University of Illinois Press
by arrangement with the Bakery, Confectionery and
Tobacco Workers International Union, 1987

Manufactured in the United States of America

1 2 3 4 5 C P 5 4 3 2 1

This book is printed on acid-free paper.

ISBN 0-252-01422-7 (cloth)
ISBN 0-252-01423-5 (paper)

ii

*To my mother, Margie Kaufman,
who knew when to send me out
to look for my first job.*

Table of Contents

Foreword
by Lane Kirkland

I n the lobby of the AFL-CIO building are two murals, two stories high and comprising more than half-a-million mosaic tiles.

Separately, no one tile does very much. But when hundreds of them are grouped together, they create the figures of working men and women; and when all of them are arranged in intricate patterns, we can appreciate the full story of labor's achievements, hopes and dreams.

So it is with the trade union movement. Each member is part of a local union, the locals make up the national and international unions, and they, in turn, give full expression to the family of labor.

This history of the Bakery and Convectionery Workers is an important part of the trade union mosaic. Spanning a century of challenge and change, it recounts the struggles of the first unionized bakers—against enormous odds—until they triumphed over adversity.

The struggle has continued for 100 years. These have not been easy years—for the B&C or for the labor movement, and all of us bear the scars to prove it.

The B&C grappled with outside forces which did their best to crush it. This union also had to come to grips with internal forces which, at times, threatened to tear it asunder.

When you read this history, you will understand why the Bakery, Confectionery and Tobacco Workers, as the organization has been known since 1978, today enjoys such widespread respect for service to its members, to all workers and to the well-being of our nation.

Lane Kirkland,
President, AFL-CIO

Introduction

This history was prepared in conjunction with the depositing of the historical records of the Bakery and Confectionery Workers International Union at the University of Maryland Archives, and in anticipation of the celebration of the Union's 100th anniversary in 1986.

It derives most heavily from information in the Union's records, the Union's official journals, extensive interviews with bakers' leaders, and the private collection of nineteenth century bakers' materials loaned to the author by Paul Brenner. During the preparation of the history the officers of the Union have extended their fullest cooperation and support. It is difficult to see how a history of this sort could have been compiled without their help. In addition the author would especially like to thank Gene Zack who, in copyediting the manuscript for this book, improved it in countless ways.

In the history of the Bakery and Confectionery Workers International Union it is easy to become impressed with complexities—with the myriad of ethnic groups it represented or the many divisions on the basis of the ideology, sex, and skill of the members and the industries in which they worked. Through all of this, however, as well as through the twelve-year split that began in 1957, key leaders have sustained a vision of unity. That vision is the inspirational thread that runs through the fabric of the Union's story.

The boycotted bakery of Mrs. Esther A. Gray at 508 Hudson Street, New York City, Daily Graphic, *April 13, 1886.*

———————— 1 ————————

Rise and Survival

Full eighteen hours under the ground, Toiling and making bread!
Shut off from air and light and sound,
Are we alive or dead?
. . .
Are we men with thought and resistless will,
Or are we but batches of dough,
That take their shape from the pan they fill?
Is what I would like to know.

(From "Song for the Bakers" by Enoch George Adams, St. Helen, Oregon, ca. 1884)

He came to the United States from Bohemia in 1867, at the age of twenty. He spent almost a decade in Philadelphia becoming a pocketbook maker, taking an active role in Socialist organizations, and working for a labor newspaper. Then, about 1877, George Block moved to New York City where he gradually found a niche as a reporter for the Socialist *New Yorker Volkszeitung*, helped found the Central Labor Union in 1882, and served as its long-time corresponding secretary. He was a labor journalist at a time when the role of the labor press was to be part of the news as well as to report it, and he used his position to organize brewers, bakers and any number of others among the German workers whose activities he reported.

It was in this capacity that Block took a leading role in 1880 in founding the Journeymen Bakers Union of New York, Brooklyn and vicinity. He estimated that there were about 5,000 bakers in New York City and another 2,000 in Brooklyn, all but a few hundred of them Germans. Some 3,200 bakers joined the union in short order. To garner public sympathy, Block published a sixteen-page pamphlet entitled "Slavery in the Baker Shops" telling the public about the "invisible" producers of their bread.

Based on a survey of 505 workers, Block's pamphlet painted a dismal picture. A baker's work week usually involved 16 hours a day for five days of the week, as much as 23 hours on Saturdays, and an additional five on Sundays. The bulk of this work took place during night hours in hot subterranean bakeries; many of the bakers suffered from rheumatism because of the regular cooling off they sought for their perspired bodies in the wintry open air. Often the workers slept right in the bakerooms or in proximity to them—a letter from a baker included with the survey described beds that were nothing more than "a heap of old rags on which for years not a ray of the sun shone, of the washing of which nobody ever thinks"— and the master baker interrupted the sleep of these workers whenever he had need of someone to unload flour, harness a horse, or carry out some other bakeshop or household task.

George Block

Surprisingly, Block's pamphlet was sympathetic toward the bosses, especially those it referred to as the "worst bloodsuckers." They were most often owners of marginal shops, individuals who had worked for years as bakers, depriving themselves to scrape together a scanty savings that might give them the first foothold on independence. Launching out by starting a shop on too little capital, they found the odds against their success almost insuperable. Against better established shops they often could compete only for the poorest of customers, having to sell to them on credit, at best waiting a while for payment, as often suffering a loss by default. Alternately, they might enter the more prosperous market by offering better merchandise at a low price only to find that their funds ran out before they were able to build a regular clientele. Bad luck with their horse and wagon, or illness and accidents, easily destroyed these fragile enterprises.

The entire process tended to create a class of small bakers who were hardened to the plight of the workers under them, for these bosses "had themselves previously to work so hard for an independence as to wean themselves entirely from sympathy with their fellow-drudges," Block wrote, while now "their own business cares and painstaking blunts their every human feeling."

Against Block's advice, the organized bakers struck on May 2, 1881: "I feared that the lack of discipline and of knowledge of the aims of labor organizations would not warrant them to risk the existence of the organization," he later explained.

The bakers demanded that their employers reduce their hours to 12 on weekdays, 14 on Saturday, abolish the system that required them to board where they worked, and engage all their workers through a union labor bureau. After a street parade, the strikers gathered at Irving Hall where the employers were supposed to meet them to accept the union's demands. While many employers did so, even more did not. "Many of the strikers, who happened to have good places, feared that they might lose them, and returned to their work," Block recounted; "others followed and the strike ended, after two week's duration, in a general stampede of deserters."

John Schudel, who immigrated in 1887 and became editor of the *Bakers' Journal* in 1897, later looked back on this early strike. Employers signed the agreement on the first day, he explained, but by the second day, bakers were returning to other unsigned shops "in droves" and, except for a small group that held out for two weeks, the strike had completely collapsed by its third day. Those employers who did accede to the union's terms during the strike quickly reversed themselves on the grounds that non-complying shops had a competitive advantage. The union evaporated, Schudel related, except for a few faithful leaders who stood guard over its sixty dollar treasury. The only change in conditions was that the master bakers began to treat their foremen more liberally, paying them extra in lieu of the compulsory board their fellow workers took at their place of work.

Several other local bakers unions that took form in the general excitement surrounding the events in New York, such as those in Chicago and Philadelphia, either disappeared or became simple benefit societies in the aftermath of the New York strike. The Chicago movement, interestingly enough, was also led by a Socialist journalist, Paul Grottkau, an editor of the *Chicagoer Arbeiter-Zeitung*. Of these early efforts, only the Newark union survived intact.

Organizations affiliated with the Order of the Knights of Labor, meanwhile, took the lead in the early 1880s in organizing among New York's English-speaking bakers. Though founded in 1869, the Knights of Labor was only beginning to emerge as a truly national movement a decade later. Its local bodies included both assemblies of mixed trades and single trades assemblies such as its bakers' affiliates. Irish bakers were the most prominent in accounts of Knights' activities in the baking trade. Michael A. McGrath, who joined the Knights of Labor in 1882 and represented the Bakers' Progressive Club in New York City's Central Labor Union, focused on American labor problems from the perspective of the Irish Land League. In 1883 he proposed that the CLU establish a land and rent league to fight landlordism in the United States. Four years later, the CLU adopted, "amid thundering applause," his demand for a 15 percent

3

decrease in their rents beginning May 1, 1886. "No matter how strikes were decided," McGrath told the CLU, "every one suffered, except these leeches known as landlords." He looked upon rent reduction as "the entering wedge of the land movement in this country."

Under McGrath, the Bakers' Progressive Club launched a campaign in 1883 to enforce the provision of the state penal code providing that no work should be performed on Sunday unless absolutely necessary. Engaging a lawyer, the club initiated a test case, but the court ruled that Sunday baking was a necessity and dismissed the complaint. The club also opened its own labor bureau in 1884 and, the following year, campaigned for the adoption of a state law to limit the hours in bakeshops to ten a day. Meanwhile, under the leadership of another Knight, John A. Kelly, the Long Island Bakers' Protective Association in 1885 was operating a labor bureau and considering establishing a cooperative bread factory.

It was in New York's Central Labor Union that Michael McGrath took measure of George Block, for the CLU was a meeting ground for Irish and German trade unionists. McGrath "watched him closely to see whether he was honest or not," and satisfied himself. He came to admire "how hard Mr. Block fought the cause of the bakers and the brewers when he was not connected with them at all, when he was a reporter on a labor paper." Then, perhaps as early as 1884, Block told McGrath that he was going to start a newspaper for German bakers. "I at first thought it ridiculous," McGrath confessed "then I thought it impossible; but he did it."

There were those among the German bakers who were equally skeptical of Block's efforts, according to Charles Iffland, who became one of Block's colleagues at about this time. Iffland himself had taken a tortuous route into the New York baking trade. Born in 1859 in Hessen-Nassau, Germany, he worked as a printer before coming to the United States in the late 1870s. After a short time in the South, he took a job as a ship baker's helper to work his way to England. He immigrated to New York about 1878, found work as a cake baker, and joined a bakers' aid society. He was not yet connected with the union when, following the strike of 1881, its remaining members decided to use the money still in the union's treasury to pay for their initiation into the bakers' aid society. To Iffland's chagrin, the society's leaders rejected the unionists' applications, fearing they might "infect" the society with the "spirit of unionism." Thereupon, Iffland resigned from the society. A short time later, while attending one of a series of meetings in 1884 for New York City bricklayers who were on strike for the nine-hour day, he met Block and joined

4

the effort to rebuild the bakers' union.

Iffland therefore was well positioned to witness and record Block's early efforts. One afternoon in the spring of 1884, Iffland later recalled, a small group of bakery workers met in a boarding house on Second Avenue and decided to renew the agitation for organizing the bakers. The following Saturday they held another meeting at the same place. The "young element," he explained, immediately took to Block's idea of establishing a journal and set out to build a bakers' newspaper fund by holding "small festivities" and placing subscription boxes in boarding houses frequented by bakers. Block himself carried on a correspondence to generate support from bakers in other cities. Some of the older members, however, were suspicious of these efforts, Iffland noted. They proposed, instead, to use the group's resources to establish a labor bureau "because one of the mnembers wanted a job as office-keeper." After some debate, both sides agreed to refer the matter to the executive board of the local union.

There were-less than three dozen unionized German bakers in New York City in 1884, organized into three sections, each of which sent three delegates to represent them in the local executive body. They voted five to four in favor of Block's proposal. The four dissenters then held a separate meeting with a few other members and formed a short lived Progressive Bakers' Union. Despite the disruption, however, Block was now free to launch a bakers' journal. The first issue of the *Deutsche-Amerikanische Baeckerzeitung* appeared on May 2, 1885, the fourth anniversary of the 1881 strike.

"The Germans are pushing things with an energy worthy of the cause," Michael McGrath announced at the end of May. "They have a mass meeting in some part of New York every Saturday night." The organizing drive that accompanied the appearance of their journal swelled the membership of the New York German bakers union before the end of the year to about 500; another 200 joined a separate Brooklyn organization. One crowded meeting on Second Avenue attracted both English- and German-speaking bakers, which McGrath took as an encouraging sign that the "barrier of nationality" was breaking down. By and large, however, the organizing campaign of 1885 began and remained German in character. While Block was aware that English-speaking bakers had their own union, he admitted "I know very little about the English organization."

From the time he founded the journal, Block made clear that he intended to use this medium to launch a national union. On September 2, culminating their 1885 campaign, the New York German bakers issued a call for a convention to be held in Pittsburgh on January 13, 1886, to establish a national bakers' union.

The universe of organized bakers in 1886 took in a wide variety of organizations, some associated with the Knights of Labor and some completely independent of it. Frank Harzbecker, the bakers' International secretary in 1901, in writing to American Federation of Labor President Samuel Gompers, recalled that the 1886 convention drew delegates from "Social clubs, Sick societies, Death benefit associations, and men who had formed some kind of a union to assist each other in finding employment for those being out of work." The common thread appears to have been ethnicity; so thoroughly

Delegates to the founding convention, Pittsburgh, January 1886.

German in character was this convention that the press initially reported the new organization's name as the "National Union of German Bakers."

It is not clear, on the other hand, exactly which German groups sent delegates to the gathering. The *Pittsburgh Daily Post* estimated that some sixty bakers attended the convention and the *Pittsburger Volksblatt* listed the names of delegates from 11 cities: Brooklyn, Buffalo, Chicago, Cincinnati, Detroit, Milwaukee, Newark, New Haven, New Orleans, New York, and St. Louis. The popular *John Swinton's Paper* said 30 cities were represented, noting that the New York union claimed to have 870 members and the Chicago union 630. Block himself recorded 14 organizations participating in the first convention, including nine trade unions, two bakers' sick and benevolent societies, and Knights of Labor assemblies from Brooklyn, Indianapolis, Milwaukee, and Pittsburgh. John Schudel later tallied 11 unions, two assemblies of the Knights of Labor, and two sick and death benefit associations. His list included Baltimore, Brooklyn, Buffalo, Chicago, Cleveland, Detroit, Indianapolis, Naugatuck Valley (Conn.), New Orleans, New York, Newark, Pittsburgh, and St. Louis. Two other cities, Boston and Kansas City, he reported, sent communications of support. The *Pittsburger Volksblatt* recorded additional messages of this sort from San Francisco and Omaha. Finally, a *Bakers' Journal* article in 1934 concluded that existing unions from the following cities participated in founding the organization: Baltimore, Boston, Bridgeport, Brooklyn, Buffalo, Chicago, Detroit, Hartford, Indianapolis, Kansas City, Louisville, Milwaukee, New Orleans, New York, Newark, Philadelphia, Pittsburgh, St. Louis, and St. Paul.

Over a five-day period the convention created the Journeymen Bakers National Union of the United States and identified its immediate objective as achieving a shorter workday. While western delegates carried instructions to commit the convention to the ten-hour day, Block was able to convince them that a 12-hour demand would be more tenable in a city like New York where, he demonstrated, bakers were working an average of 15½ hours a day. The convention resolved to achieve a work week consisting of five 12-hour days, with 14 hours on Fridays, except "in such places where it appears advisable to carry a further reduction."

In what became a contentious issue during the Bakers' early history, the delegates selected New York City as the seat of the National Executive Committee that served as the Union's governing body between conventions. In addition, they decided that in order for the committee to meet every two weeks, ts composition should be local in character, chosen by the affiliated locals in the vicinity of the headquarters. In practice this allowed the New York local to select five members of the committee, with Brooklyn and Newark each selecting one. The delegates did require, however, that all new laws that the executive committee suggested would have to pass a referendum of all the Union's locals before going before the national convention.

For its first two decades, the Union's leading officer was its National secretary—an individual with the duties of both corresponding and recording secretary. A second position carried considerable day-to-day responsibility, that of editor of the official journal, the *Deutsche–Amerikanische Baeckerzeitung,* which the New York local donated to the new national body. The journal changed its name to the *Bakers' Journal and Deutsch–Amerikanische Baeckerzeitung* when it adopted a dual language format in 1895. While the position of treasurer existed from the beginning, it does not appear to have come into its own as a major leadership position until midway through the first decade of the 20th century.

Block was the dominant figure of the Union's first years, serving as both National secretary and journal editor until 1888, and continuing to edit the journal for a year beyond that. Block returned from Pittsburgh after the first convention to preside over a period of rapid growth and solidification in the Union's ranks. In New York, for instance, his own Local 1, surged to a membership of about 1,300 by March 1886. In the middle of April, Block and the executive board of Local 1 met with a committee of the boss bakers' association, seeking a 12-hour workday during the week with a 14-hour Saturday— including a 30-minute lunch break, an end to rooming and boarding at the bakeries, and the engaging of bakers through union headquarters. As a *Bakers' Journal* article later reconstructed this meeting, the bosses' association president rejected the notion that bakery workers could room and board away from the bakeries because "the employers would have to hire detectives so their eggs and sugar would not be carried out of the bakery." Block answered his arguments in "a most unmerciful tone" and the employers' representatives stormed out, leaving the local to deal individually with each employer. From the union's point of view, the result was fairly satisfactory; by May 1 all the larger employers and at least 80 percent of all the shops agreed to the union's terms.

For leverage, whether in achieving their contract demands or organizing bakery shops, union leaders in these early years seemed to agree that the boycott was the most reliable weapon. Michael McGrath, for instance, announced in January 1885 that certain Brooklyn bakers were about to get a "dose" of the boycott "if their men do not join the society." He relished the thought in July that the local might decide to have a walking delegate, reasoning "If we had a delegate, now, he could place all of Herseman's customers, thereby giving the public, or, at least, the Union men and women, a chance to teach this purse-proud man that lesson which he so well deserves." In September, he described in detail the negotiations with one of the largest New York bakers, by his estimation worth $200,000. This man at first resisted the union's demand that he reinstate a foreman. When the union representatives told him "we belonged to a body of workingmen known as the 'C.L.U.', representing fifty different Trades Unions, who would boycott him if he did not employ a Union man," he experienced a "sudden change." Another employer, John Mallon, repented too late. Seeking to lift a boycott the Brooklyn Central Labor Union imposed in February 1886 because he had been working his men 14 hours five days a week and 20 on the sixth, he found he had to agree to pay the boycotters' expenses plus a fine of $25.

German bakers shared the same experience. When the German bakers first organized in Detroit, for instance, one of their employers promised to discharge any of his workers who joined. "But when he learned that his bread was going to be boycotted," the *Labor Leaf* reported, "he withdrew the ban, told the men to join, and promised a reduction in the hours of labor." In New York and Brooklyn, *John Swinton's Paper* explained in March 1886, "there are so many unorganized men in the trade, they resort to the boycott instead of the strike as a means of coercion." Considering the small five cent per capita tax of the Journeymen Bakers, it is not surprising that George Block told the closing session of the first convention to avoid strikes. "If heroic measures were required," Block's experience told him, "the best plan was to inaugurate a boycott."

In invoking the boycott, bakers' unions often were forced to face the wrath of judges who saw criminal conspiracy in the way they perceived that unions interfered with employers' businesses and intimidated and coerced their workers and customers. Mrs. Esther A. Gray became a local hero in the pages of the New York City English-language daily press in April 1886 as she warded off a boycott by German bakers trying to force four of her workers to join the union. Well-to-do sympathizers supported her—"every opponent of Trade Unions sent in money and advice," *John Swinton's Paper* explained—and Justice Duffy fined a succession of pickets whom the police brought before him on charges of disorderly conduct. Similar action dampened a struggle between organized bakers and several recalcitrant employers in Cincinnati in July, a court requiring five or six journeymen to post bonds of $1,000 each after their arrests "on the charge of boycotting." In the same month, New York bakers felt it necessary to confer with a lawyer before boycotting William Knodel's shop after a disagreement involving the working hours of two of his bakers. The result was a carefully drawn circular designed to avoid punishment:

Notice to all Consumers.

Boss Baker William Knodel, No. 364 Eighth avenue, has broken faith with Journeymen's Union No. 1, and threatened to assault the committee that waited on him that he should comply with the promise given by him to the Bakers' Union. The boycott is now prohibited; but every man in sympathy with Organized Labor well knows what to do when we appeal to him for support of our struggle with the above-named Baker Knodel.

Court prosecution may have complicated the use of the boycott but bakers nevertheless employed it effectively. Mrs. Gray, for instance, did in the end make her peace with the union and agree in the spring of 1887 to employ only union bakers.

Another example involved Bohemian workers at "Widow" Josephine Landgraf's bakery who went on strike in July 1886 and then boycotted the bread that German workers in the shop continued to produce. The *Workmen's Advocate* found this a classic case: "Finding herself on the high road to prosperity she forgot the occupants of the gutter, from among whom she had sprung, and conceived the brilliant idea of keeping them where they belonged." Though a court sentenced four of the boycotters to short terms in jail and fined seven others, the boycott effectively ended "Widow" Landgraf's bakery business. In September, after she had "made a present of the lean and empty shelves to her daughter," the union came to terms with the new proprietor. The daughter agreed to use the union label and the union helped her "get back the customers it drove away."

In Milwaukee during March 1886, bakers in Local 6 decided that as of May 1 they wanted to board away from their shops, work only ten hours a day at an increased rate of pay, and cease work entirely on Sundays. Members of the Boss Bakers Association agreed to abandon work on Sundays but were only willing to concede a 12-hour day and insisted that their employees board with them. The bakers struck all but three bakeries in mid-April after their bosses refused their demands, and the union instituted a boycott. "Ladies!" the strikers appealed; "consider, then, that you eat our very blood by eating the bread made by slaves." The Milwaukee Central Labor Union provided 20 wagons to help supply people with union bread so they would not have to buy from the struck shops. By the strike's second week, 38 employers had yielded.

As the Milwaukee boycott completed its first month, the nerves of some powerful individuals in the community began to fray. The *Milwaukee Sentinel* complained about boycotts over the previous six months in which "Men who could not afford to pay demands for increase in wages made upon them, and others who refused to allow their workmen to run their institutions, have been made to feel the bitter sting of the boycott...." At the same time the city council began considering an ordinance to make boycotting punishable by a fine of up to 500 dollars and imprisonment for up to two years. A few days later, Judge Mallory demonstrated that the legal system was not completely powerless even without such an ordinance. He fined a journeyman baker, August Seidel, $25 and court costs for disorderly conduct. The charge related to Seidel's persistence in distributing boycott literature outside Adolph Feinhold's bakery. According to Judge Mallory, the boycotting of Feinhold was "an outrage...the work of a lot of demogagues" and "clearly a scheme to destroy the business of a man who refused to be intimidated." Despite this succession of community pressures, however, the boycott was effective enough that by May 17, most of the strikers were able to return to work at higher pay and for fewer hours. They were not successful, however, in forcing their employers to abandon the boarding system.

The legal uncertainty surrounding the use of boycotts in this period is illustrated by the strike that began in San Francisco in May 1887. The German bakers in Local 24 and English-speaking bakers organized in Local 51 demanded a reduction in hours to 12 a day, an end to the boarding system, the payment of wages by the week rather than the month, and the union shop. While all of Local 51's shops acceded to the demands, 16 small shops and one large one under Local 24's jurisdiction resisted. The local struck these shops and instituted a boycott enforced by a $5 fine on any member caught purchasing boycotted bread. When police arrested several men for distributing boycott circulars, a local magistrate discharged them. At about the same time, however, when one of the boss bakers made "a murderous attack" on one of the boycotters, the court let the attacker go with the observation that he "had a right to knock a boycotter down."

In the course of the San Francisco struggle, employers were able

Baking at Nabisco, 1895. Courtesy, Nabisco Brands.

to break their employees' resistance by importing bakers from Germany and Austria. Recruiting strikebreakers in the East or even in Europe was a device that West Coast employers found effective time and again. Enticing newspaper advertisements lured many a young baker to the coast, John Schudel later observed, where more often than not they faced unemployment. The employers' "trick," according to Schudel, "has ever been to fill their city with unemployed bakers." Despite the 25-cent per capita assessment the Union voted at its third convention in St. Louis in March 1888 to support union agitation on the West Coast, the state of the San Francisco locals remained fragile. A 1900 report assessed that "After a short period of power in the eighties the organization of these men went to pieces owing to a stubborn opposition of the master bakers and disagreement in their own ranks."

By the end of February 1886, the Journeymen Bakers claimed 21 locals, increasing to 27 with 12,000 members by March. Block reported in March that Local 1 had lowered the hours in its shops to 12 a day, 14 on Saturdays, and "pretty nearly" succeeded in abolishing the boarding system of the cellar bakeries. The Union adopted a slightly modified version of its Newark local's label, and by June Block claimed that in New York City alone 75 shops, accounting for half the city's consumption, sold only labeled bread.

When the second convention of the Journeymen Bakers met in Chicago in January 1887, the organization comprised 45 locals, 27 of which sent delegates. On the strength of a year's experience they refined their constitution. Pleased with the $1,441.47 balance in their treasury and with Block's report that organized bakers had lowered hours by an average of almost two hours and raised wages an average of $2.13 a day, the organization resolved to achieve an 11-hour day and 13-hour Saturday during the coming year. Reflecting the growth of the Union in the New York area, the delegates felt they could now provide "a more fair and equitable representation" on the Executive Committee by allowing each of the following to elect one of its seven members: Local 1 of New York, Locals 2 and 43 of Newark jointly, Local 13 of New York, Local 22 of New York, Local 25 of Elizabeth, N.J., Local 29 of Jersey City, and Local 34 of Brooklyn. In addition they established a separate National Board of Appeals of seven members from Detroit Locals 29 and 39 to investigate and rule on appeals from Executive Committee decisions.

Despite the fact that some local assemblies became locals of the organization, it was clear from Block's address to the 1887 convention that the new Union represented a clean break from old affiliations. The Journeymen Bakers National Union, Block emphasized, was based upon the "democratic republican principle, so dear to all of us, of 'home rule.'" While the Bakers believed that the various trades should render each other mutual assistance, each should also "maintain and exercise complete autonomy and independence in the matters affecting their own trade affairs."

Leaders of the Knights of Labor initially contested this stance by engaging in what Block called "unwarrantable interference" in the Bakers' affairs, seriously diminishing the Union's effectiveness in its first year. Block claimed that the Knights of Labor's organizers had, from the beginning, attempted to convince Bakers locals in Baltimore, Boston, Indianapolis, Milwaukee, Pittsburgh, and other cities to become affiliates of the Order. As early as February 1886, he wrote Knights' General Secretary-Treasurer Fred Turner that the Bakers desired friendly relations with the Knights and did not claim exclusive jurisdiction in the bakery industry. He did not object, he told Turner, "when your organizers organize such bakers into assemblies that have no organization as yet," but any tampering with existing locals, under any pretext, could only lead to antagonism. Turner's reply was short and abrupt: "We never knew that the K. of L. was proscribed from bringing into its folds all branches of honorable toil."

From that point on, Block concluded that the Bakers would have to "place themselves on the defensive against the Order. . . ." Meaningfully, the Union voted to affiliate with the Knights' main rival, the American Federation of Labor. The AFL issued a charter of affiliation to the Bakers on February 23, 1887.

Over the next few years, the Union gradually gained ascendancy over the Knights in the baking industry, though the relationship between the two organizations varied with locality and was by no means uniformly antagonistic. In Pittsburgh, the German bakers at first affiliated with both organizations as Bakers Local 27 and Knights of Labor Local Assembly 1719. Early in May 1886, the local struck about 120 of the 200 bakeries in the Pittsburgh-Allegheny area demanding a 12-hour day and daylight hours. The bakery owners claimed that the effect of the daylight demand would be to put bread on the customers' tables 12 hours later than usual, giving them a stale product. "It would be just as sensible," one offered, "for the policemen or the men who keep up the fires in mills and factories to strike against night work."

A particular focal point was S. S. Marvin's factory. Because it produced machine-made bread the union insisted upon a 10-hour day. Marvin regarded it as an injustice to penalize him just "because we employ machinery to assist them." He decided to appeal to the executive board of the Knights of Labor regional body, District Assembly 3. After a nighttime meeting at his factory, District Master Workman Joseph J. Evans issued an order requiring the local bakers' assembly's members to return "quietly" to work on a 12-hour basis at hours of their employers' choosing. If striking workers failed to return, Evans ruled, the employers could hire whomever they wished to replace them, under the protection of the Knights of Labor. In a short speech to the bakers, he explained that the request for daylight work was unreasonable; reporters and printers worked nights to put fresh news before the consumers in the morning, and fresh bread required the same commitment. While the bakers returned to work, the German union withdrew from the Knights shortly afterwards. The Knights, however, continued to represent English-speaking bakers in the city.

Quite different was the growing strength of the Knights in Washington, D.C., where the Order dominated the labor movement throughout the 19th century's last decades. Local Assembly 2889, founded in February 1886, became the strongest bakers' local in the Knights of Labor. The Journeymen Bakers treated it gingerly, reporting its activities along with news of its own locals and cooperating with it during its campaigns and struggles, though not without an occasional chiding. Thus in August 1887, Block promised to do his best to prevent his Union's bakers from Baltimore from taking the place of striking Knights of Labor bakers in Washington, but was quick to remind the Washington assembly that the Knights had crippled Baltimore Local 12 to such an extent that more Baltimore bakers were outside the Journeymen Bakers than were in it; "many who may, therefore, come to Washington and fill the places of the strikers may not stand under the jurisdiction of the National Union at all."

A year later the Union's journal complained that though the Washington assembly had successfully abolished boarding in a recent campaign, it had conspicuously allowed one employer to continue the system. This individual, according to the journal, "enjoys the protection of a 'mixed assembly' of the K. of L.—perhaps he is a member of it," and was able to convince the district assembly that the strike against him was illegal because the district assembly had not sanctioned it. The Knights' mixed assemblies, it warned, had become the home of many employers who, "though they be entirely honest, have interests to subserve that are different to those of the workingman."

In Brooklyn, John Kelly, the leaders of the Knights' bakery workers, eyed the new Journeymen Bakers National Union with misgivings. His Long Island Bakers' Protective Association in the spring of 1886 had four sections—1,000 members—and its own walking delegate, and it was pressing for the eight-hour day. It seemed to him that the Pittsburgh convention of the Journeymen Bakers was a concoction of "pocketbook makers from one locality and saloon-keepers from another." That at least was the only reason he could find for the convention's 12-hour-day proposal, which amounted to a 74-hour week, for "any journeyman knows that 74 hours means 80 hours." Still, Kelly's group had to find a way to coexist with the Bakers' locals in Brooklyn. Its preponderant influence with the Master Bakers Association gave it the power to prod Bakers' Locals 3, 5, and 7 into a merger, a new unified organization emerging that affiliated with both the Knighthood and the Journeymen Bakers, known in the latter as Local 34.

Hard feelings over the 12-hour proposal developed in New York City as well. The Bakers' Progressive Club charged the "Nationals" with offering their services for less than the Knights and taking Knights' positions during strikes. German bakers in the Journeymen Bakers countered that they were worse off than English-speaking bakers and that a reduction to ten hours was simply "too great to think of." In that case, the Progressives responded, English-speaking bakers "may as well emigrate." Arbitration by the Central Labor Union, and the Journeymen Bakers' promise to investigate and punish instances of its members taking Progressives' jobs, appear to have allowed the issue to wash over.

Gradually, Progressive bakers' leader Michael McGrath became convinced that the bakers' future did not rest with the Knights of Labor. He had always been anxious to build a bridge between the German and English speaking branches of the trade. The difficulty he found was that when the more "able and honest" men in these societies proposed "anything to promote the general interest," they were put down as "notoriety-seekers." In character with the disunity of the time, members of the Knights of Labor came to McGrath several times to ask if they should expel George Block from the Central Labor Union. McGrath defended his counterpart and began to work more closely with him. They cooperated in a campaign in 1887 in support of bakers' legislation before the legislature, sharing the stage at Irving Hall in April with McGrath wielding the gavel while Block "in stentorian tones, vented his rage upon our unjust social conditions and exhorted his hearers to join the Redemptorists of Humanity," as *John Swinton's Paper* noted.

McGrath also knew that the Journeymen Bakers was no longer an exclusively German organization. At the time of its second convention in January 1887, in recognition that five of its 45 locals were English-speaking, the Union introduced an English page in its journal. In June 1887 it dropped this feature while beginning the publication of the news of the organization in English in *John Swinton's Paper*. In August, following the demise of *Swinton's*, the Union inaugurated a similar arrangement with the *Workmen's Advocate,* the official Socialist Labor Party paper published in New Haven, Connecticut. Finally, in July 1888, the Journeymen Bakers launched an official English language organ, the *Bakers' Journal,* under the editorship of Joseph P. McDonnell in Paterson, N.J. McGrath was among the first to write to the new journal, not only in congratulations but in caution, having heard some men say that the new publication would be used to "scourge and vilify the Knights of Labor;" knowing officers of the Union, however, he doubted they would do anything "so small." Nevertheless he took the opportunity to urge that "it is our duty to work hand in hand no matter whether we were born in Ireland, Germany, Russia or Africa."

Four months later, McGrath made a definitive break with the Knights in a startling announcement that after one or two years of studying the matter, he had concluded that "the Knights of Labor can never do anything for the bakers." In fact, he declaimed, during all of the six years he had been a member of the Order, the Knights had never done anything for the New York bakers but take their money. He claimed that James Quinn, Master Workman of District Assembly 49, flagrantly ignored the constitutional procedures in conducting the assembly's business and when not absorbed in the district assembly's own internal squabbles, had denigrated the Central Labor Union's boycott work and dismissed it as an organization that should be broken up. He related how Quinn had said that "he never saw a national union or a national district that ever did any good for the people belonging to them." McGrath concluded that it made no sense to have any further dealings with the Knights, "especially where there is a national union with two weekly papers to help to dispel the ignorance and gloom that hangs over our trade." McGrath became an active member of Bakers' Local 1, representing the local in the new New York City Central Labor Federation prior to his death in 1891.

Within the Knights, the idea of creating an alternative bakers' national organization ballooned and then burst during the late 1880s. Michael J. Bishop, a Brooklyn-born itinerant baker and cook, returned to his birthplace and joined the Knights in 1882, the same year that Michael McGrath did. Bishop was 28 years old in 1885 when, as recording secretary of bakers' Local Assembly 2872, he appealed to bakers' locals throughout the Order to open a correspondence that would allow them to share information and cooperate. In the winter of 1885-86 he moved to Haverhill, Mass., and by the spring had settled in Boston and joined Local Assembly 5296.

Bishop was recording secretary of his local assembly in September 1887 when it issued a call for a convention in Albany to begin December 19, to bring the various bread, cake and cracker bakers and confectioners assemblies of the Knights under one national charter. Twenty delegates responded, representing Colorado, Indiana, Illinois, Missouri, Michigan, Maine, Maryland, Massachusetts, Pennsylvania, the District of Columbia, and Toronto. In two days they created a national trade assembly, electing A. W. Vicars of Detroit, an English-born cake baker and foreman at Vaile and Crane's cracker factory, to head the new organization as master workman. The convention chose John Doyle of the strong Washington, D.C., local assembly as worthy foreman, and Bishop as secretary-treasurer.

Difficulty and dissension stalked the new national trade assembly in its brief career. Anton Kostor, a member of the Washington, D.C., local assembly, complained that his assembly's delegate to the Albany convention, John Doyle, had violated his instructions to develop a harmonious relationship with the Journeymen Bakers' National Union. Specificially, Doyle was to have encouraged either the creation of a common organization to which members of both factions could belong or to try to arrange a mutual recognition of union cards so that members of each could work alongside the other. Instead, Kostor learned, Secretary-Treasurer Michael Bishop was proving "bitterly opposed" to the Journeymen Bakers' National Union and intent on building up his local assembly in Boston by disrupting Locals 4 and 54. Doyle, furthermore, had solicited subscriptions for a newspaper Bishop was to have edited for the Knights' bakers, a paper that Koster claimed never appeared.

The bakers' national trade assembly even had difficulty attempting to convince Knights officials that it had enough local support to build a viable organization. Knights General Master Workman Terence Powderly apparently did not think it had such a base. The Journeyman Bakers reported that Powderly refused to issue it a charter until at least 20 local bakers' assemblies requested one. Michael Bishop himself represented a local assembly that, according to a report by Boston Local 4 in July 1887, was "near bursting up," after having called a mass meeting and had only 11 people show up.

In the meantime the Journeymen Bakers continued to show vitality, growing to an organization of 70 locals by the time its third annual convention met in St. Louis in March 1888. Its burgeoning growth, George Block explained to the delegates, convinced him that the responsibilities of the national secretary and editor of the journal must be divided. He therefore declined to stand for reelection as the organization's leader. The delegates pressed him to continue in office, but after Block had declined a second time, they elected him to another term as editor and chose August Delabar as secretary.

Delabar had risen to prominence in Local 24 in San Francisco during the strike and boycott the previous year, first as the local's "efficient secretary," then, as the strike progressed, as the local's president. He was, as one *Bakers' Journal* report described him, "a bright looking young German American who speaks English with the faintest perceptible accent and often times speaks it very eloquently." A Socialist like his predecessor, Delabar would be the Socialist Labor Party candidate for mayor of New York City in 1890.

Over the remainder of the decade the relations between the Journeymen Bakers and the Knights of Labor were more remarkable for their harmony than their conflict. In the same month that some Knights local assemblies were establishing a national bakers' assembly, all the bakers organizations in New York, Brooklyn, Jersey City, and Newark, including three bakers' assemblies, formed a central organization to work together for the abolition of Sunday work and "other nuisances disgracing the trade in these localities." Jersey City Local 29 reported the following summer that it was working "hand in hand" with the local assembly in that city and that the two organizations were preparing to hold a joint picnic. In August 1888 the *Bakers' Journal* praised the Knights of Labor men in Pittsburgh for preventing employers from supplying workers and materials to Cleveland bakeries where Journeymen Bakers' members were on strike. The journal took this as evidence that "In the natural order of things the K. of L. bakers will in time become part of the National Union...."

Accompanying these instances of cooperation was a steady attrition in the Knights' position in the trade. In his first official report, Delabar observed that there was "a movement among K. of L. assemblies of our craft to join the National Union," and that five or six assemblies would make the move shortly. A Philadelphia assembly joined the Journeymen Bakers in April 1888. Local 46 in Albany, carved out of Local Assembly 3271, prepared to sever its connection with the Knighthood in October 1888. Meanwhile, in August 1888, the Journeymen Bakers fixed its attention on Pittsburgh, where a second convention of the KOL national bakers' organization was set to convene.

Despite the uncertainty about the national trade assembly's status, and perhaps to demonstrate its underlying strength, its leaders called this convention, apparently with some optimism. The *Pittsburgh Dispatch* reported that representatives from 32 local bakers' assemblies were to be present. Ominously, however, the *Dispatch* pointed out that, despite the arrival of some delegates from the East, the convention had yet to conduct any business due to the failure of other delegates to appear, most prominently, Master Workman A. W. Vickars.

In his months in office, Vickars had tried to build up the assembly, speaking in places that he could reach without interfering with his job and issuing a circular depicting the bakers' national trade assembly as the instrument to inaugurate a new Declaration of Independence for bakers, one that would grant them "independence from all that is servile and menial, and a recognition that Labor, being the source of all wealth, should be honored." He also sought to assure Powderly that he was building up an organization consistent with the Order's highest ideals, telling him that "those who are intimately acquainted with me know that I am working for the success of *the Order* and the triumph of *its* principles, and not for a 'Union.'" Vicars was elected master workman of District Assembly 50 in early January 1888, running as the "Powderly" candidate against an anti-administration man.

Shortly before the August bakers' national trades assembly convention was to convene, however, his employer accosted him. Vicars on frequent occasions had taken leave of his work to take care of out-of-town business for the Knights, traveling to Pittsburgh and Washington, D.C., on bakers assembly matters. This time, however, his employer informed him on his return that he could no longer work there unless he abandoned his work for the Order. Vicars may have taken the message to heart; he apparently never arrived in Pittsburgh. In fact, though those present postponed the convention, first one day, then another, and finally a third, no more than four delegates ever arrived. The organization was stillborn. A year later Vicars was operating a state agency selling a line of cigars bearing the Knights of Labor label.

If the bakers' national trades assembly did not come to fruition, Delabar still had to deal with the Knights' continued presence on many a local scene, and his approach was to avoid conflict, extend help where he could, and allow time to take its course. This strategy recognized that the issues dividing the bakers' organizations were secondary to the more general struggle in which they were all engaged. In reaction to the growing organized strength of their workers, bosses in some locations were prepared by the end of the decade to adopt a more intransigent stance. In New York City and Brooklyn the large wholesale bakeries organized a pool in August 1889, declared a lockout, and would accept no worker back who did not subscribe to a new set of rules and regulations. These stated in substance that hours and wages would not be raised and each worker would deal with his employer on a one-to-one basis with no outside interference.

New York Local 1 was some 3,000 strong at the beginning of the lockout, holding closed shop agreements with all of the large shops; the employers' tactic showed how soft these numbers were. Some of the bakers went on strike, but others remained on the job and the employers easily found replacements for the strikers among the large number of unemployed bakers in the city. The union depended heavily upon a boycott which, though aggressively promoted in Brooklyn, was only indifferently carried out in New York City. In addition, most of the affected men were Germans who did not speak English and therefore confined their boycott activities to the German neighborhoods. The showcase of their efforts was a boycott of Fleischmann & Company, the yeast manufacturer, which they inaugurated under the impression that the firm had a connection with Fleishmann's Vienna Bakery. The Journeymen Bakers promoted this boycott with some determination and with the support of the American Federation of Labor until 1893. Nevertheless, within three days, the strike was for all practical purposes at an end, and by February 1890, even the leaders of the local union had signed the new rules. Local 1's membership by that point had dwindled to 27.

In the context of this dramatic defeat, it is not surprising that August Delabar rushed to Washington, D.C., in the spring of 1890 to stand shoulder to shoulder with the Knights of Labor local assembly faced with a virtually identical set of demands from its city's bakeries. There was little question that Local Assembly 2389 was committed to its affiliation with the Knighthood, if only because the Order had the strongest central organization in Washington, D.C. As the local assembly's recording secretary, J. Hazelbush, explained in July 1888, "the mere knowledge that we belong to them compels the bosses to respect us." Still, Hazelbush was one among many in the Washington, D.C., organization who welcomed closer relations with the Journeymen Bakers, and Delabar responded in kind.

Speaking before a mass meeting of the assembly in March 1890, Delabar told the members that their meeting would show their employers that the bakery workers had "other organizations standing by and assisting them" and urged them to "stand by their assembly. . . ." Assembly member John Schmidt commented appreciatively that Delabar "took in the meaning of these rules at once" and "explained them in such a manner that the most hardened rank scab could not help feeling ashamed of himself if he would touch a pen to sign his name to that document, or ironclad oath, as Mr. Delabar termed it." In 1890, the Bakers Union chartered Local 118 in Washington, D.C., an organization that Schmidt later related was "guided" by Local Assembly 2389 until 1899, by which time the Knights assembly "had lost its grip upon current affairs, owing to the advancement of trades unionism in general."

Even where relations between the Journeymen Bakers and the Knights were poor—as they were in Boston—Delabar sought to soft-pedal differences. James Beigin, secretary of Local 54 in 1888, took a jaundiced view of the activities of his Knights of Labor counterpart, Michael Bishop. He accused Bishop of attempting to break up Local 54 in order to get its members to join Local Assembly 5296. That assembly, he explained, was the base from which Bishop had attained a salaried position as statistician in District Assembly 30. Claiming that Bishop was not really a baker but a cook, he noted that if Local Assembly 5296 failed, Bishop would have to "go back to work in some cheap restaurant, a place where he belongs and not at the head of hard working, honorable men."

Delabar shared the view of many other members of the Bakers Union that "many times bakers' interests had been sacrificed in the K. of L. by sending men to adjust difficulties who knew nothing about the trade." Only "practical bakers" should attempt to adjust difficulties in the bakers' trade, Delabar said. Nevertheless, he urged the Boston members not to antagonize the Knights. Two years later, relations in Boston were still anything but satisfactory, but patience seemed on the brink of achieving its reward. Local 54's new secretary, E. J. Brucker, believed Local Assembly 5296 would be "in their glory" if Local 54 collapsed. "We have time and again tried to work in harmony with them," he reported, "but they could not see it and would only call us scabs and other pretty names." Fortunately, Brucker added, the local assembly was now on its "last legs." Michael Bishop went on to occupy the second highest national position in the Knighthood as General Worthy Foreman, but abandoned his career as a bakers' leader. He worked for four years as a successful book canvasser and life insurance solicitor, for a time published the *Boston Weekly Index*, and subsequently pursued a business venture in the West Indies.

A confectionery worker with dipped candy. Courtesy, Eastman House.

First Steps towards Business Unionism

From twelve to fourteen hours a night,
with doors and keyholes shut up tight,
The sulpher hung on the midnight air
Like the gruesome pall of a funeral pyre,
Yet refreshing breezes may gently blow
Across the hills from Buffalo.

(James Walsh, Local 277, Salem Mass., 1903)

As the 1890s began it was by no means clear what lessons bakers could draw from the experience of the previous decade. The Union consisted of 56 locals in good standing. It was beginning to expand its jurisdiction with a small presence in Canada and the first organizing of confectionery workers, and this was reflected in the decision of the fifth convention meeting in Detroit in March 1890 to change the name of the organization to the Journeymen Bakers' and Confectioners' International Union (B&C). On the other hand the New York, Newark, and Brooklyn locals were decimated and locals were in bad shape in New Orleans, Cincinnati, and St. Louis. Thirty-five locals that had received charters during the Union's short history no longer existed, including organizations in such centers as Baltimore, Milwaukee, and Minneapolis.

What is more, the track record of the local unions in negotiating improved conditions for bakers had so far proven anything but encouraging. John Schudel was amazed at how quickly employers could whittle away contract gains through everyday practices in the shop. As long as the workers raised no objections, he observed, the average master "will never pretend noticing any violation of the Union agreement." The average bakery workers' desire to please and "their caution rooted in a fear of losing their jobs" caused them to "tolerate little transgressions on their rights here and there," until their "good humoredness" turned to "sullen forebearance," Schudel remarked.

Another who described this pattern was Leo Schlemmer, a Bavarian immigrant and longtime financial secretary and business agent of Rochester Local 14. In 1939, a year after illness forced him to limit his activities, he reminisced for the Rochester *Labor Herald*, describing how ". . . the Master Bakers bought a pint of beer or the bosses gave the men something from the hip-pocket and the bakers worked another hour longer for the generosity of the Masters." Furthermore, according to Schlemmer, the immigrant Jewish bakers who poured into the industry in the last decades of the century seemed even more malleable, many of the so-called Hebrew bakeshops working under what he characterized as the "old European exploiting system as it prevailed in Russia, Poland, and Austria. . . ." He had in mind a system that included a work week of 90 to 100 hours.

How leaders evaluated the Union's position depended to some extent on cultural influences that extended back to Europe; in the 1880s that, for most bakers, meant Germany. "In the larger cities of the United States," Minnesota Labor Commissioner S. G. Powders noted in 1895, "there will always be found a few American trained bakers, and yet everywhere in the country the greater number in the craft learned the trade in a foreign country. The larger proportion acquired that trade in Germany. . . ."

Many of these German bakers brought a Socialist perspective with them. Max Hayes, long-time editor of the Socialist *Cleveland Citizen*, recalled that in 1888 Cleveland's new Local 19 was wholly composed of German-speaking bakers, many of whom had become "imbibed with principles" in Germany, Austria, and Switzerland. Hayes found it natural that the "happy-go-lucky" American workers looked to the Germans for leadership. Peter Beisel had similar recollections. Beisel came to Chicago in 1875 at the age of 17 from Hessen, Germany, having already served his apprenticeship in baking. He worked in Chicago until be became one of the casualties of the 1894 lockout, and then moved to St. Louis. There he became part of Local 15—predecessor to Local 4. He later described it as an exclusively German body, speculating that the cellar bakeries prevailing in St. Louis could not attract any but recent German immigrants. As was common of other German locals, its leaders, "those few brave men, who never lost hope and courage," had become Socialists in Germany, where they "received their education in the Labor movement."

Leaders with this background readily looked to political action to argument the Union's meager record in the economic sphere. For some, the drive to regulate the bakeries through legislation seemed a vital corollary to their more direct dealings with employers. When New York State Factory Inspector James Connolly presented his annual report on the bread baking industry in 1887, he believed that public exposure of the conditions of work in the trade would create an outcry for legislative remedy. The bakers had a bill before the legislature that year to impose a 10-hour day upon the trade and abolish Sunday work. It passed the Senate, but as the Albany *Argus* explained in June, in the Assembly it was "ground to pieces."

An unenviable legislative record only strengthened the appeal of the Socialist Labor Party for many bakers. Established parties, they reasoned, were undependable; only by electing working-class representatives could they inaugurate fundamental changes. August Delabar not only ran for mayor on the Socialist Labor ticket in 1890 but also stood staunchly on the Socialist side that year in a struggle with AFL President Samuel Gompers over the party's right to be represented in central labor bodies affiliated with the labor federation.

George Block's editorship of the Journeymen Bakers' journal ended in the midst of debate over the political direction of the Union. As late as December 25, 1887, the *New York Sun* had described Block as an individual with "black hair and mustache, a quick brain and an impulsive tongue" who was "one of the extreme trade unionists," an individual with "leanings toward state socialism." Yet Block spent his final year as editor of the *Deutsch-Amerikanische Baeckerzeitung* under fire from the Socialists for failing to support the party in the journal. The Union's 1889 Cincinnati convention tried to summarily replace him and while the membership reversed this decision, Block resigned May 1, 1889. Robert Degen edited the journal until August when the Board appointed Karl Ibsen; by the end of the year Ibsen was conducting the journal with much greater sympathy for the Socialist Labor Party.

The March 1891 B&C convention at Indianapolis represented the height of Socialist political activism in the Union. Its delegates condemned Samuel Gompers' stand on Socialist Labor Party representation and declared that "the condition of the working class cannot be permanently improved by trades organizations founded upon an exclusive trade union basis" because of the "present productive system swelling the army of the unemployed at an appalling rate, which reserve army threatens ruin to the best organized union...."

25

They endorsed the platform of the Socialist Labor Party as "the only hope of securing our rights by lawful means" and urged all members to join the party. Before the convention was over the delegates also added a new preamble to the B&C constitution laying out the class struggle and calling for the working class to defend its interests "economically as well as politically, in the shops as well as at the elections, municipal, State and national." Only George L. Horn, delegate from Local 18 in Indianapolis and secretary for the convention, voted against it.

At the same time that Delabar endorsed political action, he opposed proposals for a sick benefit for members. At the 1890 Detroit convention, he professed sympathy for members in distress but insisted that the labor movement had "too great a work before it to waste its energy with other than matters pertaining to the labor movement." His concern was that adopting such measures would drain resources that should be used for confronting "the great questions of emancipation of the working masses." While he agreed in 1891 to submit the question of a sick benefit to the members for a general vote, Delabar showed much more enthusiasm for the possibility of establishing a strike fund so the B&C would not have to depend solely upon assessments to support economic struggles. It was not until 1895 that the B&C adopted a sick and death fund, and then only on a voluntary basis.

While the 1891 convention seemed strongly committed to political action, there were undertones of disaffection with this position. Delabar referred elliptically to some locals who found the journal "too progressive" and who claimed that the officers were more interested in Socialism than in working for the interests of the members. In addition the convention displayed a lack of harmony between the general officers and the International Executive Board—as the 1890 convention had renamed the executive committee. According to Delabar the Board had made groundless accusations that he was misappropriating funds, this without ever examining his accounts. He attributed much of the problem to the decision of the 1890 convention to move the Board to Cleveland; the smaller size of this city left the selection of the Board members in the hands of a single local, in effect infecting the Board with petty and parochial intrigues. He nevertheless favored moving the headquarters to Cleveland in order to reunite the Union's leaders.

Although the B&C's Board of Appeals exonerated Delabar and the 1891 convention moved the Board to Chicago, dissension continued to plague the Union. Karl Ibsen resigned from the editorship at the convention, effective May 1, 1891, because the convention disallowed an extra weekly payment to him for putting out the English edition of the journal. The Board filled his position with Henry L. Weismann.

When the *New York World* took measure of Weismann on January 31, 1894, it described him as "...a stout young man, with fuzzy light hair on the top of his head and a little yellow mustache...." Weismann had immigrated to San Francisco from Bavaria when he was 18 and became an anarchist and an activist in the anti-Chinese movement. He learned the bakers' trade while serving three months of a six-month jail sentence in the house of corrections for his role in an aborted plan to dynamite the North Beach Woolen Mills, employer of several hundred Chinese workers. After his release, he operated a saloon that served as the bakers' headquarters and with August Delabar organized among the bakers. At the same time he and a group of anarchists formed the short-lived Pacific Nationalist Club, part of the movement inspired by Edward Bellamy's utopian novel, *Looking Backward.* Paul Grottkau met Weismann while on a visit to the West and recommended him to the International Executive Board.

Henry Weismann

Shortly after Weismann took over the editorship, the journal dramatically altered its view of the Socialist Labor Party. While Weismann had joined Delabar as a Socialist activist in the spring, by the summer both were at loggerheads with the party. In the Socialist controlled New York City Central Labor Federation, Weismann had nominated Delabar to serve as one of the two delegates to the international Socialist congress in Brussels scheduled for August. The central body did not select Delabar, however, and both Weismann and Delabar took issue with the decision to allow Lucien Saniel, the official Socialist Labor Party delegate to the Brussels congress, to act as one of the Central Labor Federation delegates as well. Three unions pulled out of the central body after the dispute—Delabar's Local 1, Weismann's cake bakers' Local 7, and Local 7 of the International Typographical Union. They eventually joined the rival Central Labor Union. By the end of the summer, B&C Local 93, which remained loyal to the Central Labor Federation, was demanding Weismann's resignation for failing to support the Socialist Labor Party in accordance with the resolutions of the 1891 B&C convention.

In short order the B&C received a second jolt when, in April 1892,

Delabar announced that he was resigning as national secretary effective May 1. The skirmishes between the secretary and the International Executive Board had continued unabated despite the transfer of the Board to Chicago. Delabar complained that the Board had continually hampered his work through disallowance of his expenditures. The Board in turn claimed that "We have been repeatedly bulldozed by an Int. Sec'y in every case where we have had a difference of opinion." Weismann acted as secretary until September 1892 when the Buffalo convention, originally scheduled for 1893, met to confront the crisis.

The convention proved a stark break with the past. George Horn of Indianapolis, the one delegate at the Indianapolis convention to vote against the new preamble, now emerged as the national secretary. Henry Weismann remained ensconced in the editorial position until 1897, as well as serving as national secretary after Horn's resignation in May 1895. The Bakers had inaugurated an administration implacably opposed to the political affiliations of the past.

A historical piece in the journal five years later, possibly written by John Schudel, would suggest that the Buffalo convention was the beginning of a new era. Until then, it argued, the Union "was practically nothing more than an experiment and the hunting ground of factions, parties and individuals, who threw only now and again a solitary crumb of comfort to the masses as a bait to catch their votes." The new administration was for him a turning toward "the simple, soul-inspiring truths that lie at the basis of the trade-union struggle; its effect on the development of human freedom; its world-shaking, revolutionary import; its force in the evolution of manliness and independence; the ideal hidden in the simplest contest for a mere raise of wages...." The key principle laid down by the 1892 convention was that the Union's laws and policies must be directed toward "strictly trade union aims" that "will shut off neither democrat nor republican, neither social democrat nor anarchist, from joining us, and working hand in hand with us for the common interest of the union."

Accompanying this reversal of the political stance of the B&C was a modest reshaping of the organization that took it on its first steps toward "business unionism." The central thrust of business unionism involved welding members together through an organization in which high dues and strict accounting procedures supported attractive benefits for them while on the job, unemployed, on strike, and in retirement. According to Lawrence Hashey, who studied the B&C's benefits system in the 1930s for his masters' thesis at North-western University, many bakers initially opposed the adoption of benefits that might appear to convert the Union into a fraternal organization rather than "a fighting organization designed to protect and better the conditions of the workers." The strike fund, however, was both a benefit and an instrument of militancy, and as such could appeal to a broader cross section of members.

The strike fund materialized at the 1892 convention as a compromise to prevent the delegates from cutting the existing dues of 25 cents per month per member. While the convention reduced the dues to 15 cents a month, it provided that the locals continue to collect the remaining ten cents to use as a strike fund. The delegates also voted to provide the locals with uniform account books. Considering that accompanying these changes the B&C for the next 18 months conducted the most intensive organizing campaign of its short history, bringing in a large number of new locals, the 1892 convention appeared to be a watershed.

Not all the Bakers' locals willingly followed in this direction. In New York City, for instance, while Locals 1 and 7, Lower East Side unions, led the pullback from the Socialist Labor Party, Local 92 on the Upper East Side and Local 93 on the West Side soon left the B&C to become the core of an independent bakers' movement committed to the party. By the beginning of 1894, the Socialist organ *People* exuded, there were 38 independent bakers' unions around the country, 11 of them in large cities. This, it concluded, was "the best proof of the widespread dissatisfaction with bankrupt sand-lotter Heinrich Weismann." On May 11, 1895, 14 delegates representing independent unions in New York, Newark, Boston, Roxbury, Newport, Brockton, and Bridgeport met at the latter city to found the Independent Bakers and Confectioners of America. They adopted the *People* and the *New Yorker Volkszeitung*, Socialist Labor Party publications, as their organs, and pledged themselves to support the platform and candidates of the party.

This ideological struggle played itself out in economically trying times. Whatever impact the B&C leaders believed their new policies would have for their members—and up to August 1893 they were claiming that their "expectations were fully realized"—they were undermined by the financial crisis of that month. Inaugurating a depression that dragged on through the mid-90s, it struck the B&C like a "thunderbolt," the *Bakers' Journal* reported; most of the new locals "went to the wall." The fear and despair that accompanied the flood of unemployed bakers willing to work for reduced wages forced many locals in smaller cities to disband, while larger locals suffered heavy losses in membership.

Symptomatic was the great Chicago lockout that began during Christmas of 1893. The Chicago German bakers had survived a period a divisiveness which saw Locals 10 and 28 withdraw from the National Union in 1887 because the National disallowed a local assessment to support the *Chicago Baecker Zeitung*. The National Union then chartered Local 49, and for four years it coexisted with the organization formed by the seceding locals, known as Independent Local 1.

Despite this division, the two Chicago bakers organizations fashioned an effective movement. John Schudel recalled in 1901 that there was "hardly ever a time in Chicago without some shop strike or other in the larger bakeries, followed by boycotts which were pursued with considerable vigor, and if they cannot be ranked with clear cut successes, the firms, every time, took the first opportunity for a settlement...." The attempt by master bakers to blacklist all Union leaders, the arrest of Local 49's leaders in 1888, and other employer-inspired actions, forced the locals to closely coordinate their own activities. Before long they were working together through a joint executive board and operating a joint labor employment bureau.

In 1888, the two German bakers unions, numbering in total about 1,000 members, together with a Bohemian and a Scandinavian union, each with 200 members, successfully struck for the abolition of the boarding system, a ten-hour work day with 12 on the sixth day, an end to bakers having to haul flour, a union shop with workers hired through the union employment office, and access to the shops by union walking delegates. In June 1891, they reduced Saturday work to ten hours. That December the German bakers merged to form B&C Local 2 while the German cake bakers formed Local 64. The following June they successfully introduced the union label in the city. The Chicago bakers were among the largest financial contributors to the New York City area bakers during their 1889 lockout and successfully prevented Detroit employers from hiring Chicago bakers during the Detroit strike of 1892 for the substitution of day work for night work.

The depression dealt the Chicago bakers a devastating blow. The Master Bakers' Association chose Christmas 1893 to announce that hereafter they would only deal with their workers as individuals and would not tolerate outside interference, that they alone would determine who would work for them and the character of the work to be done, and that only workers signing a pledge to recognize these conditions could work in their shops. Armed with their union label, which had wide support from the Trades and Labor Assembly and the Central Labor Union, and a four-page newspaper entitled the

Organizer, the Chicago locals carried on a bitter resistance for about a year before recognizing that the circumstances were "insurrmountable." Indicative of the long-range effect of this defeat, the B&C's journal in 1897 admitted that the Chicago locals were still "in a state of comparative helplessness."

In the course of this economic crisis, the B&C convened its eighth convention in Baltimore in June 1894. This convention decided to reunite the international officers and the General Executive Board, moving both to Brooklyn. It also proposed that the membership vote on instituting a sick and death benefits plan. Purely voluntary in nature, the measure provided that the support of any three members of a local union would be sufficient to establish a branch of the sick and death benefit fund. Each branch would have to engage a physician and pay for physical examinations for prospective members. For a fee of $1.25 per quarter, members in good health would be eligible for a sick benefit of $5 a week for up to 26 weeks in a year starting from the eighth day of illness. They also would receive a death benefit ranging from $50 to $100 depending upon length of service as a member in good standing, and a $50 benefit upon the death of a wife. By a narrow vote, a referendum of the general membership approved the plan in July 1895.

This level of progress was not sufficient, however, to prevent George Horn from resigning from the national secretaryship in May 1895, according to the *Bakers' Journal*, because of "his despair of the possibility of a revival." The B&C chose to economize by consolidating the positions of editor and national secretary, with Henry Weismann assuming the joint post. He did so at the very point that an era of bakeshop legislation was beginning that seemed to offer new ways to invigorate the B&C.

Between 1887 and 1890, bakers' unions in New York, Philadelphia, Boston, and Washington, D.C., had engaged in abortive campaigns for bakery regulatory laws. These unsuccessful efforts apparently discouraged further efforts for a time. In the interim, however, bakeries became an issue of public health as medical studies demonstrated how easily a loaf of bread could transmit contagious diseases. Board of health agencies in Chicago, Brooklyn, and San Francisco gathered evidence in the early 1890s. In September 1894, upon the urging of English-speaking New York Local 80, the *New York Recorder* began publishing stories and drawings depicting cellar bakeries; the *New York Press* followed suit and the exposure of bakery conditions was soon a nationwide press phenomenon. Bakery locals in Minnesota introduced a bakeshop sanitary measure early in 1895, while the New York commissioner initiated legislation in his state about the same time combining sanitary measures with a provision for the ten-hour day. The Minnesota law passed and went into effect on April 25, followed by the New York law on May 2.

One of the four state inspectors appointed under the New York law was Dennis Hanlon, president of the apparently heavily Irish B&C Local 80, who helped celebrate the local's second anniversary that year by singing an Irish American song, according to the *Bakers' Journal*, with "such vigor that he had everyone on their feet singing, and before he finished he was surrounded with the Irish and American flags." Hanlon was soon sifting through the grim 150-page 1892 report of the New York State Bureau of Labor Statistics on bakeshop conditions with a comprehension that came from having labored in bakeshops himself since he was a boy. To compile this report State Statistician Charles Fletcher Peck had enlisted union journeymen bakers, equipped with credentials from his office. Now Hanlon was responsible for confronting the conditions Peck's work had exposed.

The findings in the report confirmed that most bakers in New York City worked in cellar bakeshops in quarters suited at best for the storage of wood, coal, and household rubbish. In poorly ventilated areas, seldom higher than seven feet and often reaching temperatures of 100 to 110 degrees, they worked night shifts averaging between 13 and 14 hours. What is more, the report showed, bakers often had to board and lodge with their employers, making their beds on shop benches or in some corner of the shop under covers used for molding bread, being on call at any hour of the day. "I have known many bakeshops where the bakers in this manner rested their weary bones for months and years," Hanlon reflected, "but seldom changing their clothes, working, eating and sleeping in these surroundings with no companions, but the dogs and cats and the vermin that populate a large number of these shops."

A "knecht" was the term for such a servant in Germany, a New York State statistical report explained in 1896. According to this report, while the factory system had severed the connection between workers and their bosses' households in other trades, the menial servant remained a feature of the baking industry because of its large number of small shops. In a statewide survey of 3,253 bakers it found that 1,408 lodged and boarded with their employers that year, another 86 receiving board alone, for a total of 46 percent who "adhere to this ancient custom." Of the eight municipalities the report sampled, the boarding system was still widespread in Albany, Brooklyn, Buffalo, New York City, Rochester, Troy and Utica; only the Syracuse industry had abandoned it.

The boarding system, Bakers' representatives had told the New Jersey Bureau of Statistics of Labor and Industries in 1892, isolated workers in surroundings under their employers' control. It left them little choice in the face of disagreeable conditions but to quit and look for work elsewhere. "Shifting or roving" bakers, the Union spokesmen explained, were virtually impossible to organize and posed a persistent threat to employed bakers.

When Dennis Hanlon began making his inspection tours in 1895, conditions strained his powers of description. At a Hudson Street bakeshop, leaking sewerage flowed unnoticed into the fermentation tub, joining the yeast in the production process. At a Third Avenue shop, cesspools of putrefying water from a defective sink converted the floor into a muddy marsh, exuding odors that drove him out-doors. Amid the filth in a Ninth Avenue establishment, he watched rats milling about like domesticated animals. "Another noteworthy feature," he offered in restrained horror, "was the dense population of cockroaches, many of them the size of grasshoppers, who, not wanting to be disturbed in their unlimited reign about the oven and water closet, flew at me like birds, and I can assure you, caused my immediate retreat from that part of the shop."

Another prevalent feature of the bakers' lives in these decades was the institution known as the "bakers' home." Many bakers did not have stable employment with one employer. When unemployed

A cellar bakery, photographed by Lewis W. Hines, 1910.

or not sleeping in their bosses' shop, the bakers could avail themselves for the bakers' home, a neighborhood saloon that threw together a few beds upstairs or in a rear shanty, the saloon keeper acting as a labor contractor for those who regularly patronized the bar.

As with other systems of private unregulated labor contracting, the system was subject to serious abuse. John Schudel, assistant secretary of the B&C in 1897, told a gathering of New York City clergymen and reformers how the bakery workers paid "their tribute to the greedy proprietor" because they feared to earn his displeasure or hoped to court his help in finding work when they were unemployed. "A sober man had rarely a chance," he reflected, because a boarding house "father" would frequently use his great influence with employers to get frugal men discharged in order to force them to drink away their savings at his bar. S. G. Powders, whose first report on bakeshop inspection in Minnesota in 1895 found the cellar locations of the majority of his city's small bakeries "entirely unsuited for the purpose," confirmed that bakers' homes "gave the greatest help to those who spent the most money at the bar."

It was in the winters that bakers were most dependent upon the services of bakers' homes and most at their mercy. In the summer business was usually flush and skilled bakers' labor in demand, but in the winter work fell off, bakers from smaller towns drifted into the cities, and a large population of unemployed floating labor swelled the population of the bakers' homes. In this season the bosses usually took advantage of the pressure of a large surplus of workers. "In those years when they were unprotected by their unions," the *Bakers' Journal* later reflected, "it meant reduction of wages, coarser fare on the tables of their bosses, discharge for some, and longer hours of labor for those that remained at work."

The inspections of Dennis Hanlon and S. G. Powders were the beginning of a spate of activity. The New York and Minnesota laws served as models for other jurisdictions during the mid-1890s: Connecticut, Maryland, Massachusetts, Missouri, New Jersey, Ohio, Pennsylvania, Milwaukee, San Francisco, Ontario and British Columbia all soon enacted similar legislation and inaugurated their own inspections. These demonstrated that the conditions that Hanlon's and Powders' reports laid bare were, as John Schudel claimed, quite typical of those "in nearly every city on our continent."

Enactment of these laws seemed to provide the breakthrough the B&C's leaders needed to convince dissenting bakers that the Union was on the right track. In New York, Charles Iffland chaired a meeting of German Locals 1 and 7, Bohemian Local 22, English-speaking Local 80, Local 164 of Morisania, and Knights of Labor bakers. It appointed a committee to divide the city into agitation districts to pressure employers to comply with the new bakeshop law. The participating locals also sent a committee to invite the independent unions to the next joint meeting. By October, subcommittees were collecting statistics in 35 districts to help the bakeshop inspectors and had already visited 390 of the city's nearly 1,400 bakeshops and interviewed 925 bakers about their working conditions. By October, as well, two independent bakers unions had returned to the B&C as Locals 92 and 93. The B&C's leaders explained to the general membership that the agitation and activities associated with the passage and enforcement of the bakeshop legislation had "convinced the more intelligent bakers of New York that their place is in the International Union." During 1896, elements of the independent bakers in Boston, Brockton, Newark, and Philadelphia as well as pie bakers in New York enrolled in the B&C while those of San Francisco and Chicago simply disbanded their organizations.

Throughout the remainder of the decade, however, certain other independent bakers' unions continued and strengthened their commitment to Socialist Labor Party political action. They formed the Bakers' and Confectioners' Alliance in affiliation with the Socialist Trade and Labor Alliance, founded as the economic wing of the Socialist Labor Party in December 1985, and continued to criticize the B&C. In 1897, for instance, the Executive Board of the Bakers' Alliance argued that the old Journeymen Bakers had been stronger with a 5-cent per capita dues in the time of George Block than the B&C was with its 25-cent dues under Henry Weismann, that the expense of the journal and the $25-a-week salaries of its leaders were dragging the B&C down, and that since 1892 the B&C had shown no ability to resist the decline in wages and the increase in unemployment. The Alliance derided the benefits system of the Cigar Makers' International Union which unions like the B&C took as a model, claiming that the system only worked when there was relatively low unemployment, while it drove even the strongest unions toward bankruptcy in hard times. Finally it claimed that strikes and boycotts were bound to fail as long as the workers, led by "fakirs," elected political officials who worked to defeat them. It was not until 1900, several years into the recovery, that the core of the independent movement in New York and Boston reunited with the B&C, ending, the *Bakers' Journal* announced, "seven years of separation, antagonism, spite and bitter warfare between two phalanxes of men whose interests are the same, who suffer under the same evils...."

That an opposition of this sort was able to sustain itself doggedly for so long suggests that despite the euphoria in the B&C, bakeshop legislation was not the panacea some thought at the time of its enactment. With sense of vindication, the B&C lauded its own support for a legislator like Arthur J. Audette who had supported bakeshop legislation as well as an armload of other labor measures in the New York state assembly, all the while that the Socialist Labor Party's official papers saw fit "to antagonize, to denounce and villify Mr. Audette as an enemy of labor. . . ." When the Ohio legislature failed to appropriate funds in 1896 for the enforcement of that state's bakeshop law, the governor called a special meeting of the State Board of Emergencies which came up with enough money for two inspectors' salaries. The *Bakers' Journal* took this as an occasion to unload one of its more impressive sentences upon the Socialist Labor Party:

> Had the bakers of Ohio listened to the advice of their so-called radical friends who, when the Legislature failed to provide the funds to enforce the law, claimed that this result had been premeditated, that the law was intended to remain a dead letter, that so-called capitalist politicians were unwilling under any circumstances to grant any of the trade-unions' demands unless the latter transformed itself into a political ward club and went into hysterics over the question of that world-saving panacea, independent political party action; yes, had the bakers been taken off their feet by the verbosity of the labor politician and his doctrinaire arraignment of everything that is not wrapped into the folds of the red flag, then, indeed, would their efforts have been in vain.

In truth, the effects of the bakeshop legislation were mixed at best. On the positive side, Dennis Hanlon told the International Convention of Factory Inspectors in Detroit during September 1897, the New York law had already forced 900 shops to equip themselves with ventilating pipes and hoods above the oven doors, and 400 shops with a ceiling height of between five-and-a-half and seven feet to increase their height to eight feet or more. Shops sitting on solid rock or in buildings with shallow foundation walls or in places where the tidewater from the East and North rivers prevented digging, he explained, had added windows and airshafts to compensate.

Beyond physical improvements, Hanlon's speech exemplified the way that bakeshop laws, by creating a professional bureaucracy dedicated to bakeshop health, assured the increased dissemination of scientific and medical information on the conditions of the bakeries. On this occasion he drew attention to an article by Dr. F. J. Waldo, medical officer of health to St. George, Southwark, London, in the *Journal of the Sanitary Institute*; Waldo decribed the premature aging of bakers due to the fatiguing nature of the work and lack of sleep, the dampness, the great and suddenly fluctuating temperatures, and the breathing of an atmosphere charged with dust and coal fumes.

On the other hand, as the B&C's campaign for enforcement in New York suggests, the leaders were aware that the law could become a dead letter without the vigilance and determination of the bakers themselves to see that it was enforced. Even with such efforts, the end results were disappointing. The *Bakers' Journal* in November 1899 admitted that reports by bakeshop inspection departments tended to present their work in the best possible light and "do not generally give the true state of affairs in a trade." For the bakers' trade, the most that the journal could say was that the sanitary laws had eliminated "many an old nuisance" and that the prohibition of child labor had resulted in the use of more men in place of boys. Nevertheless, despite the best efforts of the bakers themselves, conditions were "deplorable." It was, the journal preached, a lesson in the danger of overrating what could be achieved by legislation, of believing in the "omnipotency of law."

Turn of the century wholesale bakery. Richmond, Va. Courtesy, Valentine Museum.

Joseph Schmidt, a 19-year-old Austrian baker, presented an even less sanguine assessment of the impact of the law. Schmidt had joined Local 1 when he arrived in the United States in 1894. In 1900, he wrote to the *Bakers' Journal* concerning a bill then before the New York legislature to license labor bureaus and prohibit their operating out of saloons, as was customary in the bakers boarding home system. Schmidt's six years of experience in New York taught him not to be too optimistic about relief through laws. Under the existing bakeshop legislation, he claimed, "the old dirt was daubed over and several holes were nailed down with tin-pans" but "for the rest everything has remained as it was formerly." The ten-hour clause had had no impact; new cellar bakeries continued to appear while modern ventilation and health arrangements were as elusive as ever. The blame, he believed, lay heavily with the indifference of the bakers themselves. Even the few improvements that the bakeshop law had ushered in owed their implementation "nearly exclusively" to the "indefatigable activity of the bakers' unions."

In 1905, the United States Supreme Court in the case of *Lochner v. New York* struck down the New York law limiting bakeshop hours. The decision found that the Fourteenth Amendment restricted the state from interfering in this manner with the liberty of workers to sell their labor. While the case was a landmark in constitutional history, it was merely a latter day confirmation of lessons bakers leaders had been learning for some time concerning the limits of what they could expect from legislation.

As the hope for legislative relief diminished, the B&C fell into disarray, its progress toward business unionism stalled and its leadership demoralized. Enactment of the bakeshop laws had proven only a temporary spur to membership. At the Baltimore convention in 1894, the first to present delegates with national membership figures, Secretary Horn announced that there were 4,912 members, though without indicating how many were actually in good standing. At the Cleveland convention in May 1897, the B&C had 4,623 members, 3,208 of them in good standing. The Chicago convention in 1899 showed a further decline to a membership of 3,886, only 2,871 in good standing.

Internal disagreements made the Union seem even weaker. John Schudel, who filled the new post of assisant secretary established in March 1896 and who also served as general secretary of the sick and death benefit fund, campaigned fruitlessly to make membership in the fund compulsory for all members. An 1887 immigrant and a member of Chicago Local 2, Schudel firmly believed in the priority of economic over political action. "Shop control by which the working time is regulated and which brings protection to the toiler where he suffers most oppression," he argued, "cannot be reached through politics." He saw little relationship between voting and "self-reliance, which is so necessary in men, who would be free." Only through the building up of trade unions could workers become "a power in the economic field." The key to building up the B&C, he felt, was a sound benefits system, "the agency through which our organization will attain that stability which is essential to its further growth and prosperity."

The depression only strengthened Schudel's faith in this approach. Looking back in 1901 he believed that only unions with well-established benefits features had emerged from the depression "nearly unscathed." Lacking these at the time, he judged, the B&C stagnated for the rest of the decade. Yet many members coming out of the depression would have agreed with Michael Murphy of Local 30 in Syracuse who found compulsory membership "abhorrent

Cellar baker, stairs to street at rear.

to every American citizen" and found benefits features superfluous to the functions of trade unions. Some 90 percent of the B&C's members, Murphy estimated, belonged to some benevolent association of their own ethnic or religious group and were already carrying all the insurance they needed. Out of respect for the cosmopolitan nature of the country, Murphy held, unions should stick to improving working conditions in the trades. Schudel could only counter that this reasoning was "near-sighted" and "a serious obstacle in the progress of our organization, undermining the hopes of many of our brothers in united and consolidated action."

When the 1897 Cleveland convention of the B&C adopted an out-of-work benefit to put before the general vote of the membership, it once again chose to propose a voluntary program. Schudel in turn was almost thankful when the referendum defeated the proposal, claiming that on a voluntary basis the measure would have been an "impossibility." Finding the notion of "out-of-work clubs" hopelessly narrowminded, he asked, "should we let the State or town authorities take hold of this matter, as it is done already in some parts of Germany and Switzerland? Must it also be said of the American workingmen, that they are unable to regulate this between themselves?"

John Schudel

Schudel rose to the leadership of the B&C in November 1897 following the resignation of Henry Weismann on October 15. Weismann had been drifting for some time, turning more of the administrative work over to Schudel while he studied law and launched a bakery under his wife's name. The Executive Board's growing interest in how he was transacting the financial aspects of the journal's advertising may have triggered his resignation. Following Weismann's resignation, Schudel later related, the former B&C leader and his supporters from Brooklyn attempted to seize physical possession of the B&C's headquarters in order to obliterate any record of their transactions. Fortunately, Schudel explained to the 1899 Chicago convention, members of New York City Locals 164 and 1 "sent their members to the spot of danger whenever there was occasion for their services."

Weismann's bakery failed and by early 1898 the B&C was accusing him and supporters in the Brooklyn joint executive board of attempting to launch a new journal to draw away advertisers from the B&C's journal. According to the B&C, Weismann's group intended to make the new journal the official organ of bakers' sick and death

40

benefit associations, singing societies, and clubs and to charge them a 5-cent per capita fee for the service. If successful, the next step would be to establish employment offices and resurrect the ancient bakers' trade guild. "The trade guild which still lingers in Germany and Austria," the *Bakers' Journal* warned, "is the most deathly foe to the interests of the journeymen bakers" because in it they are "blinded with ideas of equality of interests between the master bakers and themselves."

The Weismann affair produced an unprecedented demand among the locals for reform of the B&C. Plans for changing the organization's constitution poured into headquarters, overwhelming the International Executive Board. Conflicting propositions, Schudel explained, hardened into "confrontations, accompanied by bitter feelings on account of local considerations," until the leaders seized on a proposal by Local 7 to hold its next convention in 1899 rather than 1900 as scheduled.

Meeting in March 1899 in Chicago, the tenth B&C convention sought to decentralize the organization to reduce the potential for fraudulent activity. The delegates voted to once again separate the editorship from the office of international secretary. They also attempted to strengthen the participation of the rank and file by elaborating on an institution that had been with the B&C since its beginnings—the general vote. Beginning with the first constitution, all major measures approved by conventions had gone to a membership referendum. This included measures that made the purchase of the *Bakers' Journal* compulsory for all German-reading members, and that created the voluntary sick and death benefit fund. The Chicago convention, in line with Schudel's recommendation that the general vote "be made a reliable, distinct and useful institution by creating well-defined constitutional clauses for it," provided for a general vote each year on all important propositions, a simple majority determining whether or not they would become part of the constitution. In addition, the membership would nominate and elect all national officers every two years through the general vote. Each local would nominate one candidate for each office, the five individuals with the most nominations becoming the candidates, but only one candidate standing for election from any single locality.

In general, what the B&C seemed to be groping for was a way to strengthen local autonomy and control while continuing on the path to business unionism, a process usually associated with centralization. Thus, Schudel called for a "sound and plain financial system based upon the autonomy of our locals, no more money to be sent to the International headquarters than is necessary to keep

A B&C promotional calendar, 1904.

it up. . . . '' The convention's disposal of the strike fund reflected this injunction. Created by the 1894 convention by designating a portion of the International dues to be held by the locals for that purpose, it had never had adequate administrative rules to segregate it from local funds and provide for its separate management. Now the B&C abandoned the fund altogether, leaving the money in the hands of the locals despite Charles Iffland's motion to return half the sum to the International. The B&C would have to rely thereafter on special assessments to support strikes. At the same time, however, the convention recognized the continued need for high dues, providing that no local that charged less than 60-cents per month for local dues would be entitled to any support from the International.

Several other aspects of the 1899 convention furthered the decentralization of the B&C. Delegates were obviously determined to take control of the headquarters out of a locality they felt had encouraged abuse of power. When the convention met in Chicago in March 1899, Joe Schmidt later reminisced, it was all "You New Yorkers can beware! This was the welcome greeting for us on our leaving the train at the station in Chicago." As the site for the B&C's headquarters the convention nominated Boston, Cleveland, St. Louis, and New York; the membership in its general vote in July chose Cleveland. Meanwhile the delegates also accepted Schudel's suggestion to provide for the appointment of International organizers in every large city, selected from among local nominees. Finally, they put before the general vote the proposal of the International officers to institute compulsory sick and death and out-of-work benefits. The membership rejected the notion of compulsory funds in July, a decision that Schudel recognized moved the locus of activity more firmly to the local scene: "we have to be satisfied to work in this cause as heretofore, pushing local benefit funds and thereby give air and free scope for voluntary funds which will, by their natural growth, enroll, in the course of time, the largest part of our membership."

With the general vote in July 1899, Frank H. Harzbecker became International secretary, John Schudel remaining as editor of the journal. Harzbecker, a business agent from Local 4 in Boston and a successful organizer for the B&C throughout New England, had served as assistant secretary under Schudel since Henry Weismann's resignation. He took office as fundamental changes in the baking industry were beginning to drastically remake the B&C's world.

Factory and delivery wagons of Moir, Son and Co., Bakers and Confectioners, Halifax, 1907. Courtesy, Public Archives of Nova Scotia.

Search for Stability

*"A Journeyman Baker, who expects to start a small bakery in a few
weeks, tells how the* Helper *helped him to get ahead. He writes: 'I
had calls for cakes that I had never made. Most of them were clearly
explained in the* Helper *and I got along first rate.' He got better wages,
saved a little, and will soon be his own boss. The* Bakers' Helper *will
help any baker who is willing to be helped. Send for a Sample Copy."*
(From an advertisement in the Bakers' Journal, *January 1902)*

That the *Bakers' Helper* could still find it reasonable at the
turn of the century to slant its subscription advertisements
towards the bakers' hopes for going into business for themselves was a tribute to the dogged entrepreneurship that
the land of opportunity inspired.

The bulk of the industry consisted of small marginal shops in 1900
just as it had three decades earlier. In New York City before 1872,
John Schudel remembered, no bakery employed more than 20
workers; even in 1901, he added, cities such as San Francisco,
Milwaukee, St. Paul and Minneapolis had no bakery that large. Most
shops consisted of a master baker with no more than a few
journeymen.

It was an industry characterised by pockets of chance, often in
immigrant neighborhoods where, for what was still a relatively small
investment, an ambitious baker might have a try at fortune by serving the tastes of his compatriots. Jack Zamford, a Dutch immigrant
and member of San Francisco Local 24, estimated that a baker could
launch a small shop for $200. A cellar shop no doubt required less,
and the worst conditions were often found among bakeries in the
newest immigrant neighborhoods—in New York City in 1895, for
instance, at the extreme eastern, southern and western fringes of
the city in the Jewish and Italian quarters.

The organizers of the B&C understood from the very first that
their success depended upon making inroads among ethnic groups

other than the Germans who predominated in the organization. Hebrew and Bohemian locals, for example, were part of the B&C from its beginnings in 1886. New York Italian bakers organized in the 1890s in opposition to the traditional seven-day week in their bakeries, though they themselves were hampered by their inability to organize bakers in the French and Swedish shops with whom they competed.

As long as it was possible to start a small bakery on a shoestring, labor conditions reflected the desperate survival mentality of the shop owners and the willingness of their workers to abide them while awaiting their own chance to rise to shop ownership as well. "The most miserable treatment," Schudel suggested, "was made bearable through the hope in the breast of every one to settle in business at the attainable time." Primitive conditions persisted despite the determined efforts of reformers and unionists to legislate them into oblivion. So widespread was that constellation of features associated with cellar bakeries, such as the boarding and lodging system and the seven-day work week, that their challengers no longer had any illusions concerning their ability to abolish them.

The cellar bakeries affected conditions throughout the trade. In November 1894, Hebrew Bakers' Local 165 pulled 500 men out of 200 downtown shops in New York City after employers rejected the union's demand for a 12-hour day and a raise in wages for journeymen from the range of $3 to $5 a week to a range of $9 to $16. According to the employers, "they could not accede to these demands because they were obliged to compete with bakers who conducted their business in basements which were also used as living apartments, and who, consequently, paid no store rent." While the strike was successful, union advances in such an environment were often short-lived. Local 165 was forced to strike again in February 1895 in a dispute over violations of the November agreement in 120 shops, involving 400 bakers. A pattern of regular strikes developed in which locals won small improvements only to see employers whittle them away.

It was similarly difficult to deal with trade conditions legislatively. Despite constant pressure to eliminate Sunday operations through legislation, baking and sales continued in most places on the seventh day. The preference of customers for freshly baked bread in the morning, an 1885 report of the New York Bureau of Statistics of Labor suggested, was enough to force bakers generally to keep their stores open until nine or ten o'clock Sunday mornings, and to require their employees to work Saturday night and Sunday morning to stock their stores for Sunday sales.

"There is no great profit in the Sunday trade," the report claimed, "but each thinks, if he were to close on Sunday, it would result in the loss of much of the week-day custom. They do not see the necessity of keeping open on Sunday, except that people want fresh bread and their wants must be supplied." Despite a Sunday closing law, the condition remained much the same almost two decades later. "All efforts of our unions against these evils," the *Bakers' Journal* reported darkly in March 1902 concerning the law's enforcement in New York City, "resulted but in the transfer of them from one place to another. For one Sunday bakery closed, another or perhaps two are opened in another part of that vast city."

Information from cities around the country confirmed that certain conditions were stubbornly resistant to reform. In October 1897 the B&C's western organizer, for instance, found that the only difference in conditions in the poorer class of shops in St. Louis and Cincinnati was that the former worked their bakers seven days a week while the latter instead worked a six-day week that included 24 hours on Saturday. In both, "the boardinghouse system stands in full bloom, also the time honored usage of boarding the lodging with the employers." In 1900, San Francisco's bakers still worked seven days a week, 14 to 18 hours a day, and 90 percent of the shops were in "ill-ventilated, unhealthy, in some cases filthy basements." A writer from Paterson, N.J., found the boarding system still flourishing and identified the German bakers' one luxury as their singing society, composed of both employers and employees, that provided them with cheap beer and a meal every Saturday night.

Where progress against prevailing work conditions seemed to be most pronounced, it gave the leaders of the Bakers' Union small comfort. That was because it was in the larger and most union-resistant bakeries that general improvement was most noticeable. In 1899, 78 percent of the bakeries in the country still employed four or fewer employees. About 10 percent, however, were larger shops built upon several decades of steady technological development and the prospect of serving a growing urban market. The portion of the industry devoted to cracker production had mechanized earliest; by 1840 bakers of non-perishable "ships' bread" were already utilizing hand operated mixers and machines to roll out and stamp dough, expanding with the need for travelers' bread to fuel the westward migration. Expansion of operations to serve wartime needs during the Civil War was followed by the industry's conversion to the production of the popular English yeast-raised crackers and sweet crackers—cookies—and importation of advanced English methods and machinery to produce them. By 1900, the country's cracker bakeries were vitually entirely mechanized operations.

Innovation proceeded more slowly in the bread baking portion of the industry, but the introduction of the continuous firing oven in the 1870s, mechanized mixers in the 1880s, an automatic molding machine in 1888, and an automatic dough divider in 1895 meant that some big city wholesale establishments by the end of the century were producing as many as 15,000 loaves of bread a day.

At this stage there was as yet a "missing link" to complete mechanization, since bread manufacture still required the hand rounding of the dough from the divider and the subjecting of the loaves to a short interval of proofing before the molder could shape them for baking. A breakthrough came with the initial development of a crude rounder and proofer around 1905 and its improvement during the following years. For now, however, the *Bakers' Helper* could still note in 1898 that the bread molding machine was enabling Brice Baking Company of Chicago to produce 36 loaves a minute, pronouncing that "That part of the work in the manufacture of bread-making which requires most labor, which gave sustenance to the greater number of journeymen bakers can now be done by machine." It represented, according to this report, a reduction by one half in the number of bakers required for the operation. The *Bakers' Journal* could only add wishfully that this might mark the beginning of a "new epoch" for the Union by teaching bakers that "their aspirations to go into business for themselves have become a fond illusion...."

A horse-drawn bread delivery wagon.

Technological advances encouraged changes in scale and organization in the industry. Single firms that grew in size no longer could think simply in terms of a neighborhood market. Most commonly they shifted to wholesale distribution through grocery stores, providing horse and wagon delivery and developing planned routes and sales territories. They reached out by this means throughout the entire city and, with drop shipments, to outlying areas as well. Large firms tended to concentrate on bread baking to the exclusion of "fancy goods" and developed a variety of special inducements to build a stable market for their product. These included consignment selling (whereby the grocer received credit for unsold bread), price cutting, gifts to grocers, as well as special promotional gifts to purchasers. They also began to develop product lines with their own trademarks and to create a demand for them through advertising.

The development of these large wholesaling operations forced many medium sized wholesale bakeries to revert to baking exclusively for the retail trade. Without the resources to compete with the larger firms either in terms of introduction of the latest machinery or development of regular and efficient modes of delivery, they tended to drop their wagon trade soon after the large companies penetrated their neighborhoods.

In the retail trade, only the baking of cakes and "fancy goods" remained unaffected by large firm competition, this being the part of the trade that the large shops "cast aside" because it required more work and yielded lower profits. In the bread market, the 10 percent of the firms who were large producers controlled about 25 percent of the market by 1900. Their goods were now penetrating the markets of hundreds of small bakers as well as competing with the products of other large producers whose market areas they overlapped. Bakery workers witnessed the competition as a "death struggle" between larger and small producers, with the small bakeshops compelled to "fall back on the workingmen" through wage cuts, increased hours and locating their bakeries in cheap rent cellars.

Against this turn of events, the Bakers' locals in some cities came to rely increasingly on the union label. A tense exchange among union members in 1899 illustrates this emphasis. In the election of B&C officers that year, every English-speaking nominee suffered defeat. At this, E. H. Higgins of Denver Local 26 complained that the German dominated International Executive Board was a clear case of taxation without representation. To August Nuber, a board member from Chicago, the issue was different. The active members of Chicago Local 2, he explained, had agitated against English-speaking nominees because they came from Syracuse and

Washington, D.C.—cities where the locals had not introduced the Union's label. According to Nuber, "only cities where the union label predominates should be entitled to be represented on our Int. Ex. Board." While Denver might have successfully organized most of its shops without the use of the label, he acknowledged, New York and Chicago were faced with an army of unemployed bakers, a proliferation of bakers' homes and other circumstances that made shop control unthinkable without the label. The board had to have members who "have experience in that line."

The following year, the *Bakers' Journal* featured the work of Buffalo Locals 16 and 160, through whose efforts that city was using more labels than any other in the country. Both locals, it reported, were flourishing, all but a few master bakers having signed union contracts. "In consideration of the many difficulties attending the control of the hours of labor and union rules in small shops," the journal reflected, "this renewal. . .means a good deal. . . ."

On one level, the immediate beneficiaries of an effective label campaign were bound to be the traditional B&C members, small shop journeymen whose neighborhood coincided with their employers' market and who could mobilize community opinion to bolster their position in their shop. On another level, however, Union leaders recognized that expanding from their traditional base was the key to dealing with the even more formidable problem of organizing the workers in the larger bread factories whose competition was driving them to the wall.

Factory workers tended to view their own problems in relative terms. Even in his earliest inspections Dennis Hanlon found that the large factories were more pleasant places in which to work. "I find," he observed, "that the boss bakers with the exception of those whose plants are conducted on modern principles with the aid of every technical improvement which machinery can supply, are rather indifferent, if not antagonistic to the enforcement of the law. . . ."

"All wrong is comparative," the *Bakers' Journal* observed in 1902. The factories worked by "factory rules," which at least meant regular 10-hour shifts and, with steadier work, a chance to earn enough to maintain a family. Workers in the large shops become "docile factory slaves" after "drawing comparisons with the small shops around them. . . ."

Wherever large factories appeared, the nature of the work force changed along with the nature of the work. According to the United States Industrial Commission in 1901, machinery not only displaced workers—one worker doing the work of six on a mixer, for instance, or of eight to ten on a molder—but the worker operating the machine was often different in kind as well. Not only less skilled men but also women and children were taking the place of skilled bakers in many operations. John Gardner, a member of Local 204 of Toronto, wrote in November 1902 that only two "mechanics of the old school" were required in a modern factory of 50 workers. The industry was being taken over by "specialists" with less than three years of training at the trade, and there was no longer any place for a baker with "knowledge of the whole process." Gardner wondered what prospect there could be for locals who still clung to rules requiring complete training for their members. The Industrial Commission seemed to raise an equally troublesome question simply by pointing out that of 5,208 B&C members in January 1900, not a single one was a woman. The 1901 figures, showing 23 women out of 7,120 members, hardly heralded a major step forward.

These work force changes proceeded fastest in the cracker and bisquit end of the industry where business concentration moved so quickly that it apparently caught the organized bakers almost completely by surprise. At least this was the observation of Andrew A. Myrup. Born in Copenhagen in 1880, Myrup had immigrated to Racine, Wisconsin, in 1894, where he became a journeyman baker. He joined Scandinavian Local 62 of Chicago when he was 18 years old and, after three years as an itinerant baker in California, became Local 62's business representative in 1901. Six years later, the B&C's 1907 convention elected him International treasurer.

In an interview in 1913, Myrup looked back to the time when skilled bakers produced crackers alongside bread in 40 or 50 shops in Chicago and when between 5,000 and 6,000 organized workers produced crackers nationwide. Now a few isolated organized cracker workers were making what he called their last stand—a few in San Francisco, some in Peoria, and others in Brockton, Mass. "The bakers' union did not realize that this evolution was going on in the baking industry," Myrup explained, "until the cracker trust was practially enthroned and established...."

Concentration of the cracker and biscuit business came in several swift strokes in a decade from the late 1880s to the late 1890s, following years of intense competition among independent firms. Several large mergers pulled together most of the industry, creating such giants as the New York, the American, and the United States biscuit companies. The New York Biscuit Company, established in 1890 with $9 million in capital stock, had plants principally in Boston, New York, Newark, Philadelphia, and smaller locations in the Northeast, with one plant in Chicago. Its largest plant occupied an entire block in New York City at 15th Street and Ninth Avenue. The American

Biscuit Company, established about the same time, had plants in the South and West, with one plant in New York. The United States Biscuit Company operated out of the West and Midwest. While the firms did not actually divide up the territory, they did produce similar products and worked together to establish common prices. The final stroke came in 1898 with the merging of the firms along with some of the remaining independents to form the conglomerate National Biscuit Company. In its first year, the new company controlled about 70 percent of the national cracker and biscuit market.

Initially the B&C attempted to deal with the new entities as it had with smaller employers. It approached the merged organizations in the early 1890s only to be rebuffed, it explained, by a management that paid the industry's lowest wages and refused to recognize the Union. Consequently, 1896, the B&C issued a new label designed for barrels, boxes, and packages containing union-made crackers. It also appealed to the American Federation of Labor to demand that Nabisco employ only union workers. The cracker trust remained impregnable, however, union officials reporting to the United States Industrial Commission in 1901 that Nabisco continually thwarted unions by hiring "unskilled and immigrant labor" to replace strikers. The AFL's frustration was reflected in its placing Nabisco on its unfair list in 1902.

In 1902 the *Bakers' Journal* could still write optimistically about Nabisco's inherent weakness in competition with the large number of small independent manufacturers still in the field. The following year served to disabuse Bakers' leaders of this notion, however, as the Trust locked out the workers at its Chicago plant and endured six months by supplying its trade there from its factories in other cities. When it reopened the plant, it refused to hire anyone it suspected of union sympathy. In succession, it followed the same tactic at its other plants. At Philadelphia, the union reported, the company imported black workers from the South to keep its plant operating. The union issued a warning to "our colored brothers in the South" to watch out for Nabisco's "scab agents" and proclaimed that "this concern is now playing out race against race in its damnable efforts to rob the toilers of their right to organize and to thrive on the misery of the workers."

There was little, however, the Union could do to resist. Nabisco disdained the B&C's efforts to promote union labeled crackers. The conglomerate used its tremendous resources to crush out some local union plants through underselling, and to buy out others. "There may be a demand for union products," one reporter noted a decade after the Chicago lockout, "but no cracker plants can be found willing to manufacture them thereby willfully inviting the anger of the cracker trust." It continued to supplant higher paid bakers with unskilled workers, particularly women, and introduced its own internal welfare program for generating worker loyalty and undermining the appeal of the union. The Nabisco welfare plan opened halls where workers could hold dances, show moving pictures, hear lectures and conduct club meetings; furnished attractive bath rooms; equipped reading rooms for the workers' use; and established a limited benefit system. Surveillance and retribution also remained a prominent part of Nabisco's arsenal. In the summer of 1911, some of the company's workers who had belonged to the Bakers' Union prior to the 1903 lockout met secretly to discuss their outstanding grievances and decided to revive the union in their plant. Eighteen signed applications for union membership. The following day the company informed each of them that it no longer required their services.

Outside the cracker end of the industry, the B&C fared better in the first years of the century than it ever had before, aided by a period of sustained prosperity that saw trade unions across the board gain membership and stock their treasuries. Strengthened by a lowering of unemployment, bakers joined local unions in record number. From an organization of 80 locals and less than 4,000 members at the 1899 Chicago convention, the B&C blossomed to include 282 locals and over 18,000 members by the time its next convention convened in Buffalo in April 1903. In analyzing this rapid expansion, Frank Harzbecker devoted a section of his report to the convention to the role of prosperity in the B&C's advance.

The Buffalo convention recognized that the Union's expansion represented not only growth but to some extent a change in the nature of the membership as well, the Union now having some 2,000 female factory workers, for instance. The delegates voted, therefore, to adopt "the industrial form of government" by organizing workers in all the branches of the industry and changing the organization's name to Bakery and Confectionery Workers International Union to reflect the new organizational philosophy.

They also responded to ongoing difficulties with the B&C's system of organizers. Under the scheme established at the Chicago convention in 1899, the Union relied on local organizers to work on an *ad hoc* basis for the International. Most of these individuals found it difficult to break away from their jobs to agitate for the Union in some other locality for a few days. Some questioned whether the system was conducive to developing a group of organizers who "know their business" and the delegates decided that the Union's money would better be spent on a small cadre of full-time salaried organizers. For this purpose the B&C decided to establish seven districts and choose an organizer for each.

In other ways, however, old problems continued to frustrate the B&C's leaders. Committed to building the Union on the ground of high dues and benefits, they complained that except for a few flourishing locals which had for years had their own high local dues and benefits for sickness and unemployment, most locals "do not care in the least for benefit features." Changing their minds seemed a hopeless task as long as the membership was in a constantly "shifting state" and the locals were imbued with their "far-going autonomy."

At the same time, the debate over the political direction of the Union continued to fuel internal dissension. The Buffalo convention, for instance, quickly deteriorated into an embarrasing spectacle over the question of political strategy. Socialist delegates who tried and failed to commit the convention to Socialist political action, then blocked action on other proposals until another group of delegates despaired of further progress and withdrew. Deprived of a quorum, the convention adjourned without completing work on its agenda.

Internal dissension carried over into the summer as John Schudel, who had made the *Bakers' Journal* a bastion for non-political elements in the Union, came under increasing fire for his editorial censorship. Frank Harzbecker himself found it necessary to insert material in the journal without consulting Schudel and to dress the editor down in the journal's columns for interfering with the official communications of the Union leadership. When the vote on officers in the fall forced Schudel into a runoff with Joseph Schmidt for the editorship, Schudel resigned. Subsequent criticism by Board member August Nuber depicted Schudel as having become out of touch with the "veritable revolution" in production going on in the bakeshops. "He never visited a shop, a meeting or entertainment for the last few years and for the last few years secluded himself from everything," Nuber complained. "And so it was that he dished up worn out stuff copied from capitalistic papers."

While the political tone of the *Bakers' Journal* appeared to change with Schmidt's editorship, the difference was more in style than in substance. Schmidt himself had only recently argued that "grafting of political action on our Int'l Union" would not benefit the Socialist movement because a large part of the B&C membership was opposed to it. "The economic field," he had argued, "offers the organized workers points of action on which they all agree. . . ." Nevertheless, the replacement of Schudel seemed to clear the air

54

for a more searching discussion in the *Bakers' Journal* of the changes in the industry and how the Union must deal with them. In January 1904, for instance, the Journal gave intensive consideration to the place of women in the industry. Labor-saving machinery, it decided, made the entrance of woman into industry inevitable not because of her "abnormal inclination," nor "derangement of her mental taste," nor even a desire for economic independence, but for survival. It urged understanding for the entrance of "man's competitor" into the industry:

> It is all wrong to accuse her of having willfully abandoned her natural domain and the zeal for wifehood and for motherhood, when we know, that, owing to the insecurity of man's position as a wage earner and the increased cost of living, the number of men unable to find a household of their own is continually increasing, thus indicating that the avenue, once open for almost every woman for her support and at the same time for the exercise of her highest and nobles duties—the avenue of marriage—is rapidly closing up.

Similarly, in June, the journal defended the union label, urging readers to see in it more than a "technical palliative" for selling the products of union labor and benefiting the Union. Capitalists fought the label fiercely because they knew that it familiarized a large cross-section of society with the legitimate aims and objectives of trade unions and provided a stable base of support that neither lockouts nor the use of scabs could undermine. At the same time, the very agitation for the label by workers

> should awake the workingman from his long sleep to the class-consciousness, which every workingman must possess, in order to realize the duties which economically and politically the organization of his craft heaps upon him.

Programmatically, the leaders of the B&C still sought to commit the Union to business unionism. Among their highest priorities was a strike fund. Per capita dues from the expanding membership poured into headquarters at a rate that for the first time substantially outstripped the operating expenses of the International. The $40,000 on hand in 1903 demonstrated the Union's financial health and, as the journal argued in June 1904, "the capitalization of our trade and the situation bound to follow for our members makes the creation of a solid strike fund imperative." The B&C had already abandoned one strike fund after experimenting with a system under local control. Labor journalist A.M. Simons later suggested that the membership had never been troubled by establishing a strike fund but only by the central control of the fund. "Those fighting bakers," he assessed, "clung to the privilege of fighting whenever they felt like it. The union has always been strong upon local autonomy."

In the general vote of 1904, the members finally approved a new strike fund under centralized control. They empowered the International Executive Board to deny strike fund support to any strike that did not receive the Board's prior approval. This requirment paved the way for fairly thorough-going centralized control of strikes; by 1908 the B&C was routinely requiring locals to submit drafts of their contract proposals to the Board for approval in order to qualify for strike benefits during the term of the contract.

The 1904 vote showed the members' continued wariness, however. While they not only adopted a strike benefit but also, by a small majority, approved an out-of-work benefit as well, they simultaneously rejected a proposal to increase the per capita dues from 20 to 30 cents to cover the expense of the new funds. The International Executive Board decided, therefore, not to incorporate the out-of-work benefit into the constitution but to recommend the creation of such a benefit on a local-by-local basis instead. To build up the strike fund, on the other hand, the Board utilized its power of assessment to levy a tariff of 50 cents per member per month for four months, side-stepping for a time the lack of any long-term arrangement for its financing. The following year the members approved a 10-cent increase in the per capita dues to cover the fund's expenses.

The 1904 general vote was notable in several other respects. The members decided to move the B&C's headquarters to Chicago, where it would be rooted for decades to come. They also reduced the number of organizers from seven—one for each district—to a more manageable two. Meanwhile, in a continuing effort to adjust to the changing nature of the work force in their jurisdiction, the members approved the establishment of a low-cost special class of membership. Helpers in bread, cracker and candy factories could now pay one-half the per capita tax; those who did so would be entitled to one half the normal strike benefits.

A year later, the B&C's 1905 convention approved establishing separate auxiliary bodies for helpers and apprentices. Far from an egalitarian arrangement, it provided that the auxiliaries should operate under the supervision of the locals, and that the financial officer of the local should serve in the same capacity for the auxiliary as well. The auxiliaries could not take independent action on grievances but rather were to report them to the local for resolution. By the summer of 1906, Washington Local 118, Buffalo Local 16, and San Francisco Local 24 had established auxiliaries and, according to the *Bakers' Journal*, "gained a more effective control over the bakeshops."

During the next few years, the B&C continued to build on the basis of a commitment to both business unionism and political unionism, both centralized direction and respect for local autonomy. The Union's 12th convention in New York City in October 1905 reaffirmed the Union's commitment to "the emancipation of the working class from wage-slavery as advocated through Socialism." It provided for the discussion of Socialist principles in the columns of the *Bakers' Journal* and urged members to "ally themselves with the progressive forces on the political field...."

At the same time the convention overhauled the administrative structure of the B&C in a manner that attempted to more efficiently govern the growing union while maintaining the distinctive Bakers' Union tradition of decentralization and local autonomy. Since it inception, the B&C had governed itself between conventions through a Board whose members all came from the locality of the headquarters. John Schudel, for one, had found this system antiquated, describing it in January 1903 as the relic of a time when New York City was "the center and soul" of the organization. Now, he explained, locals spread throughout the country were dissatisfied because they had no representation on the International Executive Board. The 1905 convention decided to create a new seven member General Executive Board, each member coming from a different section of the country but all elected by the members at large. For day-to-day Board decisions and consultation with the officers the convention added a four-member "quorum" to the Board. Locals in Chicago were to elect the quorum members. The same convention, however, overwhelmingly rejected a proposal to compose the Board of one president and seven vice-presidents. As one delegate warned, an elected president in the B&C would have "more power than a Czar of Russia."

The B&C thus made measured progress toward assimilating its new members and meeting the requirements of modern administration within the bounds of older traditions of organization. Its leaders, however, were aware of the relative softness of the progress they had made and the ease with which the gains of the first few years of the century could slip through their fingers under altered conditions. Prosperity and growing membership, the *Bakers' Journal* observed in August 1905, would give way to the inevitable syndrome of dull trade and declining numbers. During the recurring downswings, "all that had been gained was generally lost," requiring "a renewal of the struggle" and the "complete energy of the membership to win back what had once been gained and again lost."

It was also clear that the Union still had not found the right combination of individuals capable of providing it with long-term stable leadership. The 1905 convention, after finding that the account books of the Union were so poorly kept as to be undecipherable by its finance committee, decided to develop a much tighter system of national financial accounting for the future. It appointed a special committee to audit the books and institute the new system, but within a year found that Secretary Harzbecker was still operating in "the old, go-as-you-please way...."

A complicating difficulty was the inability of Harzbecker and B&C Treasurer John Guild to work together. The quorum reported to members in October 1907 that these officers "have both neglected their duties through their craving for pleasures in preference to the interest of the International Union," and said that the two had even engaged in "fist contests in their intoxicated state." According to this report, the quorum had discussed the problem with Harzbecker a full year earlier but had decided to take no action at the time on Harzbecker's promise to do better. On September 24, 1907, however, the General Executive Board decided that conditions in the national office were still unimproved, and that Harzbecker's "absolute lack of business method in accounts" required his resignation.

Andrew Myrup

The concurrent resignation of Harzbecker and Guild paved the way for a new administration consisting of St. Louis Board member Otto E. Fischer as secretary and Andy Myrup as treasurer. Under this leadership, the business affairs of the Union became rationalized and orderly and the organization achieved an element of stability that had eluded it in the past. The new leaders sought to break the pattern of erratic membership that most recently had seen the B&C's numbers decline to 10,500 after the panic of 1907.

The *Bakers' Journal* in 1905 had bemoaned the large number of members who, because of the Union's relative strength during periods of prosperity, felt compelled to join the organization but never really became part of it. Some, it observed, simply "never become trade unionists in such a measure that they would adopt the aims and objects...as a matter of principle," while others actually were "filled with an everlasting hatred, because they were at one time forced to join the union. . . ." and would often ignore or undermine union working rules unless their local imposed a fine for such action. Naturally members with a limited loyalty to the organization were the first to abandon the union in economically depressed times when the surplus of unemployed bakers swelled and their local's bargaining power declined.

At the 13th B&C convention in Washington, D.C., in October 1908, Fischer asked the delegates to "inaugurate a system by which we can not only gain members but also by holding out certain inducements to them. . .make them stick to the organization. . . ." His key proposal along these lines won the endorsement of the delegates, as they agreed that the sick and death fund, which only a relatively small proportion of the members had joined on the voluntary basis, should be made compulsory for all who became members of the B&C after January 1, 1909. The fund was to operate under direct control of the International. Fischer was unable, on the other hand, to win their support for an out-of-work benefit designed, he suggested, to confront one of the underlying economic causes of instable membership, the chronic seasonal unemployment that bakers faced in winter. At the end of the convention, the Union's position on the proposal remained as it had been, a recommendation that local unions consider supporting their out-of-work members on a local basis.

As important to Fischer as the passage of the compulsory sick and death benefit was the stamp of approval the convention placed on two existing features of the organization. The delegates were satisfied with the three-year-old system of apportioning Board members by district. They decided that the expenses the Union entailed in periodically bringing Board members to headquarters for meetings of the full General Executive Board were fully justified by the range of information and experience that the new administrative structure placed at the Union's disposal and the efficiency with which the Union could now deal with developments far afield. In addition, the delegates saw no reason to alter the centralized management of the strike fund, deciding to leave it in the hands of the International officers despite proposals for local management by some of the largest locals.

The next three years proved to be a turning point for the B&C. It blossomed into a strong modern organization, growing to 20,394 members by the time of its 14th convention in Kansas City, Missouri, in September 1911, half of whom were members of the beneficiary fund. Opposition to the compulsory feature of the benefits had essentially disappeared. What is more, in those three years the B&C paid out almost $100,000 in strike benefits, more than doubling the expenditure of the previous three years as the Union moved through a period that seemed to its leaders one of "constant struggle."

B&C strike assistance generally was not sufficient by itself to assure victory to a local but could be effective in conjunction with well-grounded local campaigns. A comparison of strikes in Philadelphia and New York illustrates this point. In Philadelphia, events unexpectedly galvanized the city's bakers in 1910. Conditions in Philadelphia bakeries were among the worst in the country. In 1897 the *Bakers' Journal* claimed that the seven-day work week was more prevalent in Philadelphia than in any other city with the possible exception of San Francisco. In 1907, it commented that workers in the small shops of the city "under the whip and spur of their 'masters,' exist, or vegetate under conditions reminding one of those in the good old guild times. . . the beauty of seven workdays a week and the comfort of boarding with 'the boss'. . ." In 1907, only about three hundred of the more than 1,000 bakery workers in the city were unionized, and the few large factories that dominated the industry remained impregnable to unionization.

The Philadelphia general strike of 1910 brought the city's bakers out in support of striking streetcar workers and provided an opportunity for the International to support its local in trying to expand its base. The B&C stationed one of its general organizers, Charles Iffland, in the city from the beginning of the strike. One mass meeting drew over 1,000 bakers, including the entire work force of one of the largest bakeries, the latter vowing not to return to work unless the factory unionized. As the strike progressed, the B&C quorum donated $500 to the strikers and sent in Charles Hohmann, the former *New Yorker Volkszeitung* reporter who had taken Joseph Schmidt's place as editor of the *Bakers' Journal* in May 1908. Members of Locals 6 and 201 drew more than $3,000 in strike benefits for the period from March 5 to March 26 that they were on strike. In the end, however, the B&C recognized that the struggle had achieved no lasting results.

Charles Hohmann

The most successful campaigns in these years, on the other hand, were among locals whose members identified strongly with one another and whose leaders were able to build bridges to other working class and middle class organizations in their localities.

Such was the case, for instance, among the Jewish locals of New York City.

Bakers on parade, 1909.

The organizer for these locals was not a baker but rather a former raincoat maker from Boston. Jacob Goldstone had been born in Riga, Russia, in 1871 and had immigrated to Scotland in 1887, working first in the raincoat trade and then in the manufacture of other products for the ship-building industry. In 1895, he immigrated to Boston where he organized unions among the cloak makers, dress makers, and shirt waist workers. His attention was drawn to the bakers through an incident he witnessed one night in a crowded quarter of Boston's Jewish district. A baker collapsed and died there in front of his oven; apparently he had willingly suffered the gradual increase in his hours for the little extra it would earn him toward bringing his family to the United States from abroad. His employer, understanding the baker's ambition, had taken advantage of the situation to keep him at work for shifts extending as much as 36 hours at a time. When the baker died, the employer had one of his drivers load him onto a bakery wagon and drive him away. Goldstone was in the crowd that gathered around the wagon, among the throng who raised their hands to swear an oath to never again buy a loaf of bread that did not bear the union label. He became an organizer of B&C Local 45 of Boston, founded in 1904. In 1906, the Jewish bakers of Brooklyn and New York drafted him as their organizer.

Goldstone entered the New York scene, one observer recollected, "at a time when the union-hating Jewish boss bakers believed they had the organization of their employes about down and out." Another remembered how the bakers came to headquarters "with dough still on their hands, flour on their shoes," to sign up for the union. The locals developed a tradition of sharing work with unemployed members, giving up one or more days a week so that out-of-work brothers could sustain their families; sometimes they had to strike to force employers to agree to accept the substitutes the union sent for steady men. When strike actions came, the locals drew on the feelings of mutuality that this tradition fostered among the workers, and the members of the Jewish locals developed a reputation for not breaking ranks during such struggles. They were able, as well, to draw on their connections within the Jewish community to sustain them during strikes. The Jewish locals were closely allied with the United Hebrew Trades and received solid support from the Jewish press, particularly *Forwards* and *Warheit*.

Under these circumstances the strike and lockout of 1909 in New York City became a great consolidating action in which several hundred Jewish bakers, both organized and unorganized, toughed out two months of sometimes bloody encounters. The employers hired "sluggers," police patrolled in front of the struck shops, and at times the union's headquarters resembled a hospital. Goldstone at one point became exhausted and had to retire for a time to his home in Boston. Charles Iffland worked through Mary Dreier of the Women's Trade Union League and ultimately through Rabbi Stephen Wise to arrange a successful end to the strike, the bakers earning union recognition, a nine-hour day, and wages ranging from $12 to $25 a week. In such an environment, the $5,334 in strike benefits that the B&C paid to the 244 union members played an important role in the victory.

While the changes in the B&C were enabling it to play a growing role in support of the locals, the initiative at the end of the decade still lay with the locals themselves. For the time, members were more likely to be conscious of the uniqueness of their local situations than of a commonality that required some overarching strategy. The challenge of local companies and local events was the drama of local union life. In 1910, for instance, Denver Local 26 was just coming out of a long slumber that followed its participation in the general strike of 1903 in sympathy with the cooks' and waiters' union. In a short strike in 1910 it won the nine-hour day for its members, but at the time the members elected Ray E. Lowderback business representative in September, the local still consisted of only 60 members and a treasury of slightly more than $100. At about the same time, New Orleans Local 35, which had gradually built its membership up to a little above 300 during the decade, struck against the seven-day week and for wage increases and other improvements in conditions. A general strike of bakeries involving 305 men in 59 shops was only partially successful; it achieved the shorter work day but cost the union about 90 percent of its members. In St. Louis, Local 15 from 1908 on was locked in battle with the American Baking Company; Cincinnati Local 213 similarly engaged Kroger Bakery, beginning with a strike in 1909. Chicago's locals undertook a three-year campaign culminating in the successful enactment of a city ordinance against cellar bakeries in 1910, only to face the retaliation of the master bakers focused on a test lockout at Bremner Baking Company. It was in this contest that a company man shot and killed Charles Cerny of Local 2 after Cerny had successfully persuaded strikebreakers to stay away from the plant.

All the time, however, basic structural changes were taking place in the baking industry. The time was rapidly approaching when the intensity of local events would less easily obscure the need for a broader strategy within the B&C. Within the first year of the next decade, B&C leaders recognized they were faced with a challenge of an entirely new magnitude, one that tested the viability of the Union as a whole.

WALL STREET

NON-UNION BILLION DOLLAR COMBINE

With Millions of
Watered Stock Means
MORE WATER IN BREAD
HIGHER PRICES TO CONSUMERS
More Exploitation of the Bakery Workers

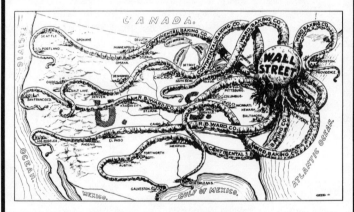

Buy only Union Label Bread and Cakes

Made in Your Home Locality Without

Wall Street Control

The Bakers' Union Label

Anti-trust poster.

4

Rise of the Trusts

"It is only your good will which we need to scotch this tyrant bread combine. If you will refuse to buy or eat its products we will win a big victory and the people will teach a lesson to arrogant monopolists." (From a Bakers' Union leaflet appealing to the people of St. Louis during a strike against the American Baking Company in February 1915)

A s early as 1905, the daily press frequently reported on an impending formation of a giant bread trust, a conglomerate organization of the type that had already appeared in such industries as oil and steel, that would merge competitors and control larger markets in the interest of stability and higher profits. It did not yet exist, the B&C's leaders satisfied themselves in February, but they had little doubt they would face such an entity in the very near future. At mid-decade, the large bakery wholesalers still represented the expansion of individual firms and, in its very recent origins, large scale production did not seem to the B&C's leaders to have had time to undermine "the sympathy which the buying public has for the small business men. . . ."

Prior to 1907, the major organizational innovation in the baking end of the industry was not fueled by merger but rather by grocery chain owner B. H. Kroger's desire to produce bread for his 42-store mid-western grocery chain by founding the Kroger Grocery and Baking Company in 1901. In 1907, however, the American Baking Company was created through the merger of seven St. Louis market area firms. A similar single market merger in 1910 brought together 12 wholesale firms in Brooklyn, New York City, and Mt. Vernon, New York, and Hoboken, New Jersey, to form the Shults Bread Company. These companies established what became an increasingly pronounced pattern in the industry.

Both the Shults enterprise and the first multi-market merger the following year that produced the General Baking Company with plants in 17 cities strung out from Boston to St. Louis and New Orleans, had roots in the so-called New York bakers' pool. Operating since the bakers' lockout in New York City in 1889, the pool had 21 years of experience in facilitating secret arrangements among the larger firms to regulate the bread market and mute competition among themselves. Through the pool, these firms supplied each other with bread during strikes, fixed prices to the detriment of smaller bakeries, and arranged for joint bulk purchasing of flour at reduced cost. Its very success helped attract the capital that now enabled firms in the pool to join in more formal ties among themselves and with firms in other localities. General Baking thus incorporated, among others, the McKinney Bread Company of St. Louis, "a notorious scab firm" according to J. L. Engdahl in *The Coming Nation*.

Of different origins was the Ward Baking Company that emerged in the summer of 1911, at about the same time as the General. The Ward Company was the project of William B. Ward, son of a Pittsburgh bakery owner, who moved to Buffalo in 1912 and began building his own baking empire with funds reputed to flow from backers in the steel industry. In a breathtaking expansion, the Ward Company went from an initial capitalization of $5 million to become a $35 million enterprise a little over a year later. In 1913 it controlled the patent rights to the Duhrkop oven, apparently the best of its day, held an interest in J. H. Day Company, a multi-state manufacturer of baking equipment, was tied to Corby Yeast Company of Washington, D.C., operated its own automobile factory— the Ward Motor Vehicle Company—to build its own delivery vehicles, and was constructing a school to train bakers for its plants.

Ward's most valuable property was its trademark, Tip-Top Bread. Out of a series of huge factories ranging from the Bronx and Brooklyn in the New York City area, to New England plants in Providence and Boston, one in Pittsburgh, two in Chicago, and another in Cleveland, the heavily promoted bread spread out on rail lines to saturate areas within two hours of the big cities. In order to extend itself into as many major markets as possible, the company licensed local independent bakeries to produce its national brand in cities and towns where it had no plants of its own. "The independent, ambitious baker sees visions showing him to be the big, particular bread trust magnate of his own city," J. L. Engdahl observed.

Once a baker signed a contract to produce Tip-Top, Ward sent in a skilled demonstrator with the Tip-Top recipe, a consignment of Tip-Top labels and a contingent of Ward marketers. They blanketed the city with billboard and newspaper advertisements, strategically located electric signs, and even large moving electrical music boxes resembling circus calliopes. Sometimes they gave out free bread for a promotional period to develop a demand for the product. Then, in a pattern that became familiar nationwide, Ward would either find a pretext to nullify its contract with the independent bakery, or simply wait until the contract's expiration, and then offer to buy out the shop. It usually succeeded through the threat to withdraw the use of the Tip-Top name. Paralleling Ward's Tip Top, other trust brands such as Butter Nut, Butter Krust, and Pan Dandy spread through the market place on the heels of a similar seductive strategy.

From the union point of view, the spread of the Trust meant a loss of jobs. For one thing, trust operations usually supplied bread from the most mechanized factories. The plant that Ward operated in Cleveland in 1911 had not had machinery six years earlier. After Ward's conversion, the work force shrunk from 70 skilled bakers to 30 workers, only six of whom were "practical" bakers. The remainder were unskilled men and boys. Similarly, the Ward plant in Pittsburgh in 1911 was operating mostly with unskilled labor earning wages of 15 to 19 cents per hour or $8 to $10 a week. What is more, according to B&C organizer Herman Ross, the Pittsburgh plant was shipping extensively into "every little village and camp" in the surrounding area, "taking the bread and living away today from hundreds of little bakers that formerly did business in a square way and employed hundreds of bakers."

Officially, the B&C did not oppose the advent of the Trust. That, the *Bakers' Journal* confessed, would be "donquixotism on our part." Centralized enterprise was here to stay, it acknowledged. What the Union wanted was recognition. "We want to safeguard the position so far gained by our organization," it insisted, "and we do not intend to permit any combination of capitalists, who seek to control the bread industry for their own benefit, to subject their workers to such damnable conditions as are now existing in the various non-union factories controlled by the very gentlemen who are seemingly so very much interested in the formation of the trust."

Trust plants, however, proved to be bastions of anti-unionism. Conditions at the Ward-Mackey Company in Pittsburgh were typical. One of the largest of the Ward plants, it discharged a driver in October 1912 apparently because company agents observed him entering union headquarters. The workers were sufficiently sobered by the experience that B&C organizers found them reluctant to talk

67

among themselves about the union and unwilling to meet with union officials except in secrecy.

These conditions became more confounding with the advent of welfare capitalism in the industry as epitomized by the so-called "Ward Idea." Launched in June 1913, this program under the Ward Department of Employes' Welfare debuted as an effort by the company to "look after the more private needs" of its workers. Ward siphoned off 6 percent of its annual excess profits over and above stockholders' profits for a fund to sustain the Ward Baking Company Beneficial Association. Through the association, it explained, "the discouraged man or woman will be encouraged, the sick member of the household given that attention which will make for restoration; the injured or invalid child will be provided with outings and medical care. . . ." The company also provided annual cash payments to reward employees for continuous service, as well as a profit-sharing plan. Any worker who left prior to serving for one full year was ineligible for profit sharing, as was any worker dismissed for inefficiency or "conduct or habits prejudicial to the interests of the company."

B&C organizers looked at bakery company paternalism with a jaundiced eye, well-acquainted with the poor general working conditions that the welfare program helped to sustain. The Memphis Bread Company, while denying in 1913 that it was part of the Ward Trust, manufactured Tip Top bread and adopted a company welfare approach to its employees, both clear indications to B&C Local 65 that it was "part and parcel" of the Trust. Two times each month, the company spent about $65 to treat its workers to an entertainment and dance at which all refreshments were free. "Think of those ignoramuses!" B&C organizer Marcel Wille anguished, "slaving and sweating their last drop of blood out for six days a week, and then going and dancing in the very same shop on the seventh day, and thinking that the boss is the best man in the world."

In trust shops on the West Coast, Charles D. Shields of Los Angeles reported in 1915, foremen made between $35 and $70 a week and several key individuals under the foreman received wages he considered fair by union standards. The majority of workers, however, known as bench and machine hands, worked ten to 14 hours a day for between $10 and $15 a week. A report on the Trust in New England about the same time indicated that boys were working on machines for between $7 and $9 a week for ten to 11 hours a day with no pay for overtime. This compared to wages in union shops in the area of $15 to $25 a week with nine-hour work days and extra pay for overtime.

68

Before 1911, the B&C developed no grand strategy for dealing with the increasing consolidation of the baking industry. It supported local initiatives and responded to local crises as they arose, providing what support it could in the way of organizers and assistance from the strike fund. Because the Trust affected the industry in the East and Midwest before it "invaded" the West, Andy Myrup did take the unusual step of visiting the West Coast locals in the summer of 1911 to warn them of the Trust's "ingenious tricks." One Portland member, while delighted with his first opportunity to meet an International officer and appreciating Myrup's information, made clear that Western locals were more concerned at the moment with the flooding of their cities with Eastern bakers, lured by false advertisements of unscrupulous employment agents. He urged that "our executive officers become familiar with the members and the conditions throughout the country" and hoped to see more of them on the road "instead of keeping them caged up in the office shooting our troubles at them at long range."

The Trust was, nevertheless, a problem of national scope, one from which even the West could not long insolate itself. By 1911, the acceleration of trust-building had jolted the B&C into developing a more general offensive strategy. Along with the emergence that year of the Ward and General baking companies, 78 leading independent cracker, bread and candy manufacturers joined to form the new Federal Biscuit Company with operations in 30 states. At the same time the Canada Bread Company absorbed three bakeries in Toronto and one in Winnipeg with a combined output of over one million loaves per week.

A candy packaging operation at the turn of the century.

Meeting in Kansas City in 1911, the 14th convention of the B&C strengthened the Union's administration and made preparations for the first time to combat the trusts on a more general level. The convention expanded the General Executive Board to 13 by adding two new districts. It also geared up for expanded activities by increasing the number of regular International organizers to three and adding an international officer; it divided the office of secretary to create two separate posts, a financial secretary and a corresponding and recording secretary, who, along with the treasurer and the editor of the journal would constitute the central leadership of the B&C. To enhance the stability and continuity of leadership, the convention expanded the officers' terms from two to three years and took over the function of nominating officers for election by the general vote. The officers also received an increase in salary. Following a general vote early the following year, Charles Iffland became recording and

Charles Iffland

corresponding secretary in February, Otto Fischer continuing as financial secretary, Andy Myrup as treasurer, and Charles Hohmann as editor.

Finally, the 1911 convention designed a broad agitation plan to confront the trustification of the industry in the marketplace. The plan was actually an expansion of a strategy already in place among New York City area locals. In the spring of 1911, an agitation committee elected by various locals that were members of the bakers' Joint Executive Board of Greater New York resolved, on Charles Iffland's urging, to push the B&C's label more vigorously through mass meetings and close cooperation with progressive and Socialist women's organizations. In July, more than 10,000 bakery workers from New York, Connecticut and New Jersey established an anti-bread trust campaign conference to coordinate anti-trust agitation and label promotion. The 1911 convention resolved to raise dues by 15 cents per month for full members and five cents for auxiliary members to sustain and expand this agitation, and in March, the B&C chose five geographical areas from which to launch the broadened campaign. The five localities included the vicinities surrounding New York, Cleveland, the Boston-Providence area, Pittsburgh and St. Louis. To coordinate their campaigns, each received a full-time B&C organizer. At the same time, the International headquarters flooded the continent with throusands of circular letters, pressing representatives of organized labor and central bodies in communities throughout the United States and Canada to avoid trust products and purchase union baked goods.

Traditions of local power and autonomy and of weak national leadership did not die easily in the B&C. Here, at the crest of its new wave of strengthened national leadership and aggressive centralized activity against the Trust, the leadership of the International suddenly found itself faced with a widespread resistance that congealed in early 1912 into a revolt. Leading the opposition were members of Chicago Local 2, for several years previous the largest and most powerful local in the International with 1,700 members and control of practically every large shop and five-sixths of the small ones in its jurisdiction. In a struggle that became increasingly acrimonious, Local 2 publicized the claim of one of its delegates to the 1911 convention, Hugo Nitz, that Andy Myrup had physically assaulted him during a debate of a special convention committee considering funding the New York and St. Louis anti-trust campaigns. The subsequent efforts of what the International claimed was a small but well-placed clique in Local 2 to have locals ignore the election of officers nominated by the 1911 convention ended January 1912 with the International revoking the local's charter and then reorganizing the local in January 1912. The International and the Chicago group reconciled a few months later after a special investigation by a committee of non-Chicago Board members exonerated the B&C leaders, leading to a retraction of all "malicious accusations" and "derogatory statements" by two key members of the Chicago group.

Local 2, however, was only the vanguard of a movement to rescind the new dues and the administrative changes of the 1911 convention. Charles W. Barth, secretary of

OUT OF REACH OF THE POOR
THANKS TO THE BREAD TRUST

Anti-Trust Cartoon, **Bakers' Journal and Deutsche-Amerikanische Baeckerzeitung,** *April 1, 1911.*

the Joint Committee of New York, spoke for many members when he suggested that high International dues would not be necessary except for the leaders' "high-styled and expensive administration." In May 1912, a general vote on the measures approved at the 1911 convention threw the leadership into despair. While barely approving the increase in dues, the expansion of the number of districts and the increase in organizers, the members struck down the provision for a new secretary's post as well as the officers' pay raise and the expansion of their terms of office.

At this point Myrup, Fischer, Hohmann and Iffland, the latter holding a position technically abolished by the general vote, decided on a bold move that permanently shifted the center of power within the B&C to the International headquarters. They announced that their "manhood" would compel them to resign if the International implemented the negative decisions of the referendum. In July, a second general vote approved the remaining measures, convincingly acceding to a new direction with the four firmly in charge in terms of power and responsibility. The victory was not without its scars, however. New York City area Locals 1, 3, and 164 engaged in a bitter campaign against the new direction of the B&C that finally resulted in their expulsion from the International in April 1913. While the B&C chartered new locals under their numbers, these organizations continued to operate as independents for the next 22 years.

In the years after the 1911 convention, the B&C was extensively involved in promoting the anti-trust campaign. Because the skill of the baker was no longer required in the factories, Andy Myrup claimed in March 1913, strikes could no longer be effective. That was why, he explained, the "entire strength of the bakery workers' organization lies in and is based upon the arousing of public sentiment...." And as Charles Iffland stressed in 1915, this could no longer be accomplished simply by agitating "in the small ranks of the labor movement surrounding us" as they had in the past; it could only succeed by reaching all bread consumers.

The obstacles to the campaign, however, were considerable. Even on New York City's Lower East Side, among people who had long preferred rye bread, nearly every grocery store stocked Tip Tip bread, lured by the larger profits for retailers that Ward built into its pricing structure. Furthermore, as the trusts were quick to demonstrate, they were fully prepared to respond aggressively to union inroads on their turf.

In the Brownsville section of Brooklyn, the Jewish bakers of Local 87 in 1910 prevailed upon grocers to stop handling the bread of the

Shults Bread Company, claiming that the Trust used lard or grease in its loaves in violation of the kosher laws. They also resolved not to allow delivery of union-made bread to groceries that handled the bread of the Trust. The union stationed pickets outside stores it suspected of handling the boycotted product and ordered union wagons away from stores whose owners were proven trust customers. Throughout the winter months they endured bad weather, arrests, and litigation, sustained by the satisfaction that came from seeing the steady spread of union cards in store windows with warnings to trust bread salesmen to keep away.

Shults responded by side-stepping the grocers and selling rye and kosher bread door-to-door, selling nickel loaves at two or three for five cents, sometimes distributing them free. The bakers kept special committees on the trust salesmen's tails, replacing these with fresh men every three hours, interrupting trust drivers in the middle of their sales pitches to tell the housewives about the conditions under which Shults made its bread. "I can assure you," one baker wrote to the B&C, "a great many don't buy after hearing that it is scab bread, and even sometimes finish up with a broomstick or a boiling kettle of hot water on the too ambitious salesman, who is sometimes glad to escape minus his basket and bread. . . ."

Agitation spread to Jewish neighborhoods of Brooklyn, the East Side, Harlem and the Bronx, grocery store owners pledging to sell only labeled bread. The United Hebrew Trades, representing some 96 locals of various crafts with a combined membership of 125,000, joined forces with the bakers, holding special label agitation meetings every other Friday. Moving picture proprietors displayed the label on their screens. The members of the locals paid all expenses through weekly assessments. Reflecting the tension and tenacity of the struggle, union members in Brownsville in the fall of 1911 were absorbing the "slugging methods" of the trust agents, several winding up in the hospital in serious condition.

Brownsville represented one strong point along the trenches for the Union, a place where it could dish out as much as it took. Another was Buffalo where, in its struggle with the union, the General Baking Company spent $100,000 on promotion, including special high commissions to grocery stores handling its product, an extensive advertising campaign in the daily newspapers, and gifts of roller skates as premiums to the customers. Still, union agitation cut into its business seriously enough to send General scrambling for business in outlying areas. All was not peaceful in the hinterland either, however. When the company shipped bread from Buffalo to Erie, it incited 43 bakeries in that town to organize a self-protection association that launched an effective "made in Erie" movement against the imported loaves.

In some towns, the Union found itself simply outmanned. This was true of some of the smaller cities along the New Haven & Hartford Railroad, for instance, where the B&C had no locals at all and Ward bread from New York and Providence found easy access to the consumer's table. It would not pay, the International decided, to send organizers into these localities. It fell back, therefore, on encouraging locals in neighboring areas to expand their jurisdiction and send their organizers into adjacent towns. If it became necessary, the B&C promised, it would send an organizer to reinforce these efforts once a local had made some progress on the scene.

In Chicago, the central office of the B&C took on a new look as it engaged in continual correspondence with leaders of regional antitrust agitation, covered the continent with circular letters, and more closely than ever monitored the affairs of the locals. Quorum members found themselves meeting four or five times a month rather than two as previously, to transact the mounting business of coordination and supervision. The B&C's leaders developed a policy of corresponding with locals whenever they seemed lethargic in their agitation or their members dilatory in attending meetings or paying their dues. This intervention, International officials believed, proved time and again to be the encouragement locals needed to inspire them to renewed activity.

The B&C's officers more intently than ever oversaw the contract negotiations of the locals, insisting that local unions must receive Board permission before resorting to strikes, and responding to local impasses by dispatching an International representative to assist the local to reach a favorable agreement without resort to a strike. By this "persistent policy," the Executive Board explained to the 15th B&C convention in Milwaukee in September 1914, the International avoided "numerous threatened and apparently unavoidable strikes." By 1916, the Board was carefully scrutinizing proposed contracts in the early spring of each year, submitted in triplicate by the locals; only provisions in approved contracts would then be defended by the B&C's strike reserve.

Gradually, B&C locals began to have success with the largest firms. Early in 1913, Local 4 in St. Louis, along with local butchers' and teamsters' unions, took on the multi-store Kroger operation in the city. The St. Louis bakers were determined upon revenge for earlier defeats that Kroger inflicted on B&C locals in Cincinnati and Dayton. "Every day some of our pickets are shoved off the sidewalks and taken to police stations to discourage the men on the picket line," organizer Herman Ross reported in March. Kroger utilized the racial division in St. Louis to its advantage by bringing in black drivers to man its delivery wagons. Three weeks into the strike the teamsters returned to work, Teamsters' national President Dan Tobin explaining that "The teamsters and drivers come in contact with all other interests and trades, and if we start in to pull out our membership in sympathetic strikes there will be no end to the conflicts we would engage in." An increasingly effective boycott supported by the Central Trades and Labor Union of St. Louis, however, began to have its effect. The Kroger stores in St. Louis were "not making expenses," Ross reported in April, and the company's desperation was reflected in the use of "slugging methods" by individual store managers. After 13 weeks, Kroger capitulated.

St. Louis bakers built upon this success in the next few years and in early 1916 reaped a bumper crop. McKinney Bread Company, a branch of General Baking, signed an agreement in March 1916. Three months later, the American Bakery Company gave in to a well-organized boycott. These trust branches adopted the standard union terms for the city: use of the label, a weekly scale of $19 for oven hands, $17 for assistants, an eight-our day with overtime at the rate of 60 cents per hour for journeymen, 40 for helpers or apprentices. On July Fourth, Local 4 held its largest parade to date, 800 members in white hats and white shirts, green neckties and black trousers, with three bands and organizer Pete Beisel on a white horse—an hour-and-a-half march followed by a grand picnic at Riverside Park lasting until midnight.

At the same time, the B&C achieved a momentous breakthrough as the four Ward plants in Chicago and a fifth in Newark signed agreements. Coupled with the signing of the New Jersey plant of Atlantic & Pacific Tea Company, which was readying its transportation department to ship union labeled bread into Ward's New York and Connecticut domain, the International found itself for the first time contemplating the possibility of the entire Ward empire soon coming to terms. These successes raised the B&C to an entirely new plane.

There were, nevertheless, still many weak points to temper the euphoria at Union headquarters. The B&C had decided at its 1914 convention to concentrate its trust agitation on a single area, choosing Boston and vicinity. Jack Zamford led the organizing effort but found that many locals were anything but cooperative, doing "more to hamper this movement than to assist. . . ." The Executive Board traced this behavior back to the manner in which the locals had first organized. Many of them had congealed only under the "organizing clubs" of the label and the boycott, Executive Board members ruminated at their March 1916 meeting. This had the effect of "compelling the men to join on account of our agitation." New locals in New Bedford, Fall River, Worcester, Lowell and Richburg quickly became "inactive and useless" because their members "lack the spirit and interest in organization." By contrast, locals in Lawrence and Haverhill, "brought into existence direct by the men in the shops," were proving to be solid and permanent bodies.

In back of Board members' minds, as well, was an understanding that the growing European war was an incalculable factor in what was happening in the industry, perhaps more responsible for the B&C's recent successes than anyone at headquarters wanted to admit. The industry was faced both with instabililty in the price and supply of raw materials and the potential of a veritable bonanza if it could maneuver itself into a position to take advantage of the wartime demand for its product. In this setting, labor peace might be

Boyer's Market, Sioux City, Iowa, refused to handle the bread of firms the bakers were striking in May 1917.

76

worth buying right now, especially where the Union was strong enough to disrupt markets. How sustainable would these union advances be, however, once the world crisis subsided? Besides, the war itself had already proven a fickle friend. In Canada, where local members were first to go off to the front in large numbers, six locals were wiped out over night, one each in Edmonton, Moose Jaw, Medicine Hat, Toronto, Hamilton and London. The remaining four— two in Montreal, one in Winnipeg and one in Toronto—were decimated and inactive.

Whatever reservations there might have been in 1916 were soon overwhelmed by the requirements and rhetoric of the war, itself. Industry and Union observers watched intently as Herbert Hoover assumed the post of Food Administrator in the spring of 1917. All indications were that he would impose extensive regulations upon the baking industry in order to economize scarce resources. The B&C hastened to petition the government to solicit the Union's advice before introducing regulations that could affect the baking trade "in a disastrous manner."

The first government order was not comforting, however. Bakers were to use no more than three pounds each of sugar and fats with each barrel of flour. In effect, the enforcement of this regulation would eliminate all sweet goods. Andy Myrup rushed off to Washington to press the Bakers' case and returned reassured; the regulation would apply only to the mixing of bread dough.

A second regulation buoyed the Union's leaders because it eradicated a practice they for some time had recognized as a bane to bakers: the system of taking back stale bread that grocery stores had not been able to sell. Employers in practice had required workers to replace these loaves without pay, claiming that they could not absorb these losses and still make a profit. In Charles Iffland's mind, the practice had always been associated with bakeries in which the worst conditions prevailed.

Of direct benefit to the industry was the movement to divert bread baking from the family kitchen to the professional bakery where the government had control over the conservation of ingredients. The goal of the movement was to rechannel 60 percent of the bread that had been baked at home to the commercial bakeries. This added a moral and patriotic imperative to the general increase in commercialization of households that accompanied the higher level of employment of women outside the home during the war; the movement reinforced the increased demand upon which the wartime baking industry thrived.

In 1917, the Ward Baking Company refused to renew its agreement with bakers in its Newark plant and locked out its workers. Faced with the adamancy of Chicago Locals 2 and 13, representing its other organized plants, Ward backed down after two weeks. In addition, after several days of negotiations, it consented to sign an agreement covering its remaining nine plants, extending to these workers the eight-hour day as well as union wages and conditions. The company's official explanation acknowledged the "gradual change which has been taking place in the public attitude toward labor" and referred to a "growing sentiment in favor of union organization" among state and national political figures and in the press. It was consistent with the company's "well-known policy of progress" and "sound business principles" to keep abreast of the times. The company was also responding to the "extraordinary conditions which today confront our country" and the splendid example of labor's patriotism in "nationally adopting resolutions abolishing during the time of war all strike propaganda and strikes." Finally, it suggested in one sweeping inspiration, that the company's new policy was a permanent one because "the time is not far distant when all labor and industry, brought to a clearer understanding of each other's ideas and ideals by the exigencies of war, will lay aside all selfish interests and unite their endeavors for the common good of all. . . ."

Wartime ideals aside, however, prosperity was the lubricant of wartime labor relations in baking. A reflection of this prosperity, at its highest level, was the estimated 27 percent profits Ward Baking earned during the war years. It loosened the purse strings when the Union sought to renegotiate wages to keep up with extraordinary wartime inflation. In October 1917, Ward voluntarily increased its wages by slightly more than 10 percent without solicitation by the Union at all. In April 1918, it negotiated another 10-percent increase, bringing its dough mixers and oven hands up to a minimum wage of $24 weekly, with bench hands, machine hands, and other journeymen bakers earning $22, apprentices beginning at $12 and helpers earning $18. During 1918, the B&C adopted a policy of recommending that locals submit questions of wage increases to their employers "in a peaceable manner. . . without opening the agreement," and found that with the exception of a single increase, employers were quite willing to raise wages by $2 to $3 a week.

Wartime did, however, create some exceptional problems for bakers' unions. The International had to launch an energetic campaign in Canada under Organizer Joseph Walsh to restore a semblance of organization in the face of the manpower drain. As with United States employers, however, their Canadian counterparts often found it desirable to settle without long strikes that might sabotage the unusual opportunities of the war period. Walsh was successful in Brantford, London and Ottawa, and reported he was more hampered by the competition of the nationalistic Canadian Federation of Labour than he was by recalcitrant bosses.

Unions were also concerned that the new workers in their plants might lower the standards they had established for their rank-and-file. John Weber, leader of Washington, D.C., Local 118, wrote in the fall of 1918 that some of his members balked when the first woman entered a local pie bakery. They all walked out, and only returned to work after the company sent the woman away. Pie firms in Washington complained of discrimination to the U.S. Department of Labor, however, and a department conciliator was able to work out an agreement in principle. The union recognized that the employment of women was inevitable in these plants, since the government had classified the baking of pies and cakes "non-essential," making male pie and cake bakers between the ages of 18 and 45 eligible for the draft. The union agreed not to object to the employment of women on the condition that they received $4.50 for an eight-hour day and that the firms established separate wash and dressing rooms for them.

Local 118 also made clear that it considered the women to be temporary replacements, establishing a separate auxiliary for them. In this way, Weber summarized, "I believe we have laid down a basis on which it will be safe for Local No. 118 to have women take the places of men in bakeries, until the men come back from the war." This action reflected a broad sentiment in the B&C. The 16th B&C convention at Boston in 1917 provided that members returning from military service after the war would immediately take their former places, and by 1918, the B&C reported that more than a thousand members who had joined the military service had taken out withdrawal cards "which guarantees that—if they are still alive—they will again return to our ranks as union men."

Another problem that dogged the Union during the war years was the German ethnicity of many bakers. In 1918, consumers began noticing what appeared to be glass splinters or ground glass in their bakery products, and rumors sensationalized by daily press coverage soon had the B&C on the defensive. One state legislature began considering a bill to bar all persons of foreign birth from any work involving the preparation of food. The International secured testimony from two instructors of chemistry at the baking department of the Chicago Lane Technical High School demonstrating that the particles in the bread related to new ingredients bakers were utilizing to conserve food resources. Corn flour, the experts explained, had many flinty pieces of endosperm that were glasslike in appearance, and bran flours contained particles of the hard outer husk that were slimy in appearance. Still, throughout the war, B&C locals had to live with the popular hysteria. Local 118 lost 35 members who were not citizens and therefore considered bad security risks for the nation's capital. Locals went out of their way, therefore, to stress the number of gold stars decorating their service flags, indicating members who had fallen in battle, and the amount of their contributions to the Red Cross and their investments in Liberty Bonds.

Henry Koch

At the end of the war, the B&C stood at a pinnacle of success. Since the expansion of the number of executive officers to four, only one individual had stepped down—Otto Fischer not standing for reelection in the 1915 general vote. Taking his place as financial secretary was Henry Koch. A German immigrant and former president of Local 195 of Paterson, New Jersey, and secretary of the New Jersey State Branch of the AFL, Koch would hold the position for the next 20 years. The quadrumverate form of leadership, with Myrup—more and more the individual the others looked upon as the main leader—Iffland, Hohmann and Koch, was providing the B&C with a long elusive stability at the top.

The Union could be proud of having accounted well for itself in some very difficult recent situations. It supported 800 bakers and helpers in a long, drawn-out general strike led by Local 6 in Philadelphia. Lasting from the end of April through the summer of 1919, it was, by the Union's calculation, one of the "most vicious fights" the B&C had ever undertaken. The *Bakers' Journal* described a "reign of terror" against pickets by company thugs in collusion with the police. If the strike failed to crack the large and notoriously anti-union firms like Kolb's and Freihofer's, it at least produced the local's first closed shop agreements in the city, affecting 150 workers.

The following year, with the help of Otto Fischer—now a B&C organizer—and financial aid from the International, Local 35 in New Orleans undertook a general strike that lasted through the spring and into the summer. Company emissaries visited strikers' homes offering them higher wages and bonuses to return to work. Several members suffered beatings while passing out strike circulars or had to face down company men "flashing guns and the like." The union reinforced its pickets and toughed it out. About 75 percent of the shops, primarily the smaller ones, acceded to the union's demands for the eight-hour day and a small raise in wages.

At the 17th B&C convention at Cincinnati in September 1920, the B&C represented 27,709 members in good standing, with another 11,000 or so on the books but in arrears. Virtually all locals had achieved the eight-hour day, except for the most recently organized, who were working nine. Reflecting the continued growth in the number of factory workers, the delegates decided no longer to make any distinction in dues and benefits among journeymen, helpers and apprentices. From now on all members, regardless of skill or sex, would pay the same monthly dues, with local unions required to charge a minimum of $1.75 per month for beneficiary members and 50 cents less for non-beneficiary members.

The leaders of the B&C were aware, however, that while the Union had adjusted well to the unusual opportunities and exigencies of the war, much had not changed during these years of crisis. If Ward Baking Company had shown itself willing to experiment with union representation, General Baking Company remained as resistant as ever, despite the best efforts of the Union under what should have been the most advantageous of conditions. When the B&C began its campaign in Philadelphia in 1918, General immediately granted workers in its Kolb plants higher wages and improved working conditions.

The General Executive Board, 1918-20; Left to Right. Front Row: R. C. Schneider, Andrew Myrup, Charles Iffland, Henry Koch, Charles Hohmann, and William McGuern; Middle Row: Frank Schneider, John Geiger, Joseph Hofer, Henry Lipkin, and Max Freund; Back Row: L. J. Martin, Christ Hansen, Herman Winter, Seb Ollinger, and Ruby Kern.

In Rochester, Local 14 had widespread support from American, Polish, German and Jewish ethnic organizations, the *Rochester Labor Herald,* the Rochester Trades Council and the Society for the Prevention of Cruelty to Children. Its strike of General's plants there stretched through the bitter winter months of early 1918, pickets braving the frost as well as intimidation by hired detectives and police. Strikers' families suffered from scarce fuel and high living costs, often under the duress of threats of eviction from homes owned by General. They watched the company making do with inexperienced Italian day laborers, and waited for a break that never came. By the end of the war, Local 14's Hebrew and Polish branches had organized 100 percent of the workers in Jewish and Polish bakeries, its Irish branch was approaching that record, and all the larger non-trust bakeries were working with the union; General was isolated but seemingly as invulnerable as ever. The Company even survived the competition of Ward bread bearing the union label, dampening this challenge in Boston, for instance, by a clever advertising campaign in which the company gave bond that its Bond bread was pure.

The B&C had also had a hard time making convincing inroads in the South. As far back as 1903, Organizer Rudolf Schirra had complained from Norfolk, Virginia, of the ability of bakery owners to play off black and white bakers against each other, their strategy being "Leave the men of each color have a separate union, get them fighting one another, then they will not have time to think or talk about bettering their conditions." Marcel Wille, in his first assignment as a B&C organizer in the South, wrote from Memphis in 1913 that it was "very funny to me for our men working six days a week alongside of a negro and then refuse to recognize him as a union man." Joseph Walsh, reporting from Richmond in June 1916, noted that as a general practice "The boss catered more to the colored baker than he did to the white, knowing that it is a hard proposition to organize the colored baker...." In November of that year, Birmingham, Alabama, bakery owners used black strike-breakers in their struggle with B&C Local 113, while in the following April in Baltimore, a marginally Southern city, employers confronted a general strike of Local 209 by using bakery wagon drivers on the production line while filling the drivers' places with blacks.

Taking advantage of racial divisions among bakers was a tactic not confined to Southern owners; in 1916 alone, such instances could be found in operations as widespread as the James Butler Grocery Store Company in Brooklyn and the Campbell Baking Company in Des Moines, Iowa. Nowhere, however, did it as uniformly undermine the B&C's efforts as it did in the South. Except in New Orleans, where Local 35 had "opened its doors" to blacks in 1918, "being confronted with the inflexible fact that there were and are to this day a hundred or more colored bakers workng at the trade," the International had found it impossible to bridge the color line. In the South, the General Executive Board told the B&C's 1920 convention, "this situation broke up every local union which had been organized."

For many within the B&C, finding a "realistic" solution to the racial problem was a troublesome compromise of their own personal liberalism. There were inspiring examples of interracial brotherhood in the B&C. The helpers auxiliary of Chicago Local 2, for instance, took pains to send one white and one black delegate to the 1920 convention in Cincinnati because its membership consisted of bakers of both races and it felt both should be represented. The convention itself demonstrated its racial solidarity when a manager of Keith's Theatre in Cincinnati barred two black bakers' convention delegates from entering with their white counterparts. The group accosted the manager to press its indignation, a committee of the convention made a follow up visit, and the theater manager, though unmoved, agreed to make a full refund on the group's tickets. Nevertheless, the convention decided to adopt the policy "practiced by most all trades in the southern part of the country," of granting separate charters to black and white locals wherever either race desired this arrangement, hoping this would increase the effectiveness of its Southern organizing campaigns.

Even as the B&C attempted to build upon its wartime successes, the return to a peacetime economy was unraveling the new fabric of labor-management relations in the industry. For years, the B&C's leaders had embraced an assumption that, in industrial relations, "The time when only one party had the say . . . is happily a thing of the past. . . ." If anything, the war had elevated this to an article of faith. As the postwar industry was beginning to demonstrate, however, it was an article written in sand, not stone.

"What's all this that's in the papers about the open shop?" asked Mr. Hennessey.

"Why, don't ye know?" asked Mr. Dooley. "Really, I'm surprised at yer ignorance, Hinnissey. What is th' open shop? Sure, 'tis where they kape the doors open to accommodate th' constant stream av' min comin' in t' take jobs cheaper than th' min what has th' jobs.... And who gits th' benefits? Thrue, it saves th' boss money, but he don't care no more f'r money think he does for his right eye.

"It's all principle wid him. He hates t' see min robbed av their indipindence, regardless av anything else."

"But," said Mr. Hennessey, "these open shop min ye menshun say they are f'r unions iv properly conducted."

"Shure," said Mr. Dooley, "iv properly conducted. An't there we are: An't how would they have them conducted? No strikes, no rules, no contracts, no scales, hardly iny wages an' dam few mimbers."
(From "Mr. Dooley and Mr. Hennessey" by Peter Finley Dunne, 1920)

Window bakeries, popular after WWI, allowed the public to view the sanitary conditions under which union bake shops operated.

5

Era of the Open Shop

In the wake of the war to make the world safe for democracy, a war to define American democracy played itself out in domestic affairs as well, in a country looking for something called "normalcy." Mirroring the United States Justice Department's purge of radical organizations were a host of local institutions from the police to vigilantes who conducted campaigns of their own against groups they identified as challenges to the American way of life. As aggressively, businessmen shaped what they presented as a distinctly "American" plan of labor relations, centered on the open shop and the democratic freedom of choice it supposedly assured workers to join or not join unions.

The American Plan swept through the baking industry in 1920. Members of Local 111 of Dallas conceded virtually all the wage and hour demands of their city's four large bakeries but found themselves forced nevertheless to strike in May to maintain their closed shop. The strike disrupted a 20-year pattern of peaceful relations in the industry. Employer lockouts closed shops in Sioux Falls and Fargo in the Dakotas. A large number of New England's locals went out at the same time. Local 11 in New Haven reported it was "entirely out" and "fighting for recognition, which the employers absolutely refuse." Many of Local 11's bakers found work in better paying occupations and the two largest bakeries signed in September after the B&C prepared to strike other plants of these companies in ten cities across Connecticut and Massachusetts.

An employers' association known as the Associated Industries promoted the American Plan in the major cities along the Pacific Coast, with equally disruptive results. Local 114 of Portland began the year as a big, powerful union that had maintained the union shop for 20 years; the employers' resistance practically put the organization out of existence. From San Diego, Los Angeles, Sacramento and Stockton to Tacoma and Victoria, locals struck, according to the B&C, after employers met their demands with "ridiculous and impossible" counterproposals.

Hundreds struck in Seattle, Executive Board member William McGuern reporting that the union had found out that "no matter what kind of an agreement the locals would have submitted this year, a strike was to be forced upon them. . . ." Most shops in Seattle reached successful settlements by the end of the summer, but Local 9 in the city sustained 85 strikers until the following April at a cost of about $20,000. Vancouver's Local 468 struck against the open shop; in the strike's sixth week it was buoyed by the news that Toronto workers had secured a favorable contract. "Many of the bakers in Vancouver," a correspondent explained, "are formerly from Toronto;" the Toronto settlement "had the effect to stiffen their pride." In 1921, however, the master bakers succeeded in smashing the union, inaugurating a decade of low wages and long hours.

Storm center for this period of confrontation was Chicago. The city had already been the site of a tense struggle in 1919 when, after six weeks of fruitless negotiations, the bakers struck the big baking companies demanding the abolition of night work. The union carried on the fight under the duress of press accusations that its leaders were "alien enemies" and "Bolsheviks," as well as an injunction from the Superior Court of Cook County against picketing or interfering with the conduct of business at the struck bakeries. That strike had ended in July 1919 after two months, with the unions conceding the night work issue and the companies agreeing to pay a 20-cents-an-hour premium for all work between 11 p.m. and 5 a.m.

By 1920, Chicago was the home of the open shop movement's headquarters, the American Press Bureau opening there in November as the general news service of the national open shop campaign. Chicago bakers must have braced themselves when they read some of the material from the bureau, particularly an interview with the manager of the St. Louis plant of the General Baking Company, George N. Meissner. He claimed that the price of bread was artificially high because of the bakers' union. The public, Meissner claimed, could only expect cheaper bread once the current agreements expired in the spring and the open shop came to prevail in the industry.

86

The open shop offensive in Chicago began in 1921 at the Ward Baking Company. One of the curious features of the national agreement between the B&C and Ward was that it did not include the Chicago and Newark locals. These locals consummated their agreements with Ward independently, well before the rest, and preferred to continue to deal autonomously with the company, despite steadfast appeals by the International. "The thought of our International Union," Charles Hohmann later explained, "was the probability that if ever at some time a break should occur between the corporation and our organization then a united stand could be made by all local unions, if all were covered by a national agreement." Instead, Ward was in a position to shake loose from some of the more entrenched locals without risking the closure of all of its plants at once.

On June 1, 1921, Ward joined the largest bakeshops in Chicago, united through the Chicago Bakers' Club, in ending their connection with B&C Local 2. The workers responded by striking. While the press carried on what the B&C called a "conspiracy of silence" concerning the strikers' activities, sluggers and managers of the companies attempted to keep their plants clear of pickets. Local 2 reached out for the support of public opinion by printing thousands of leaflets each day and seeing to their distribution. Out-of-town sister locals worked to keep scabs out of Chicago. The Illinois State Federation of Labor appealed to communities in the Illinois mining centers to boycott non-union brands. In Aurora, Local 188, with the aid of the central labor body, instituted a boycott against all products of Ward and the Schulze Baking Company.

In August, the strike reached its peak of intensity. On the sixth of the month, an individual acting as a deputy stopped the car of Henry Pfab of Local 2, and shot him in the abdomen. Pfab died of the wounds. His body lay in state at the union-owned headquarters building, a hundred singers of the Chicago Bakers Singing Society and another singing society called "Freiheit" intoned "A Son of the People I Have Always Been," and a procession of thousands with a band and drum and fife corps accompanied his body in mourning and bitterness to the Montrose Crematory.

On August 17th, detectives under the direction of the state's attorney of Cook County raided Local 2's headquarters and arrested all the local officials as well as 40 unemployed men who were on hand. They confiscated the local's books, documents and labels. The authorities grilled these prisoners for as long as 24 hours, did not allow them to communicate with relatives and friends, and finally retained 16 on charges of conspiracy. Eventually the state's attorney asked for indictments of 42, with bail set at $3,000 each. Wealthy brick manufacturer, Tom Carey, posted bail out of sympathy with the bakers' cause. In July 1922, after a defense by Clarence Darrow and Hope Thompson, the court dismissed charges against all but two, who received fines of $350 each after pleading guilty to some of the charges.

In the end, while the union won over most of the small shops, the larger shops represented by the Bakers' Club successfully introduced the open shop. The termination of the union scale in the large shops in turn exerted competitive pressure on the wages in the shops that did sign with the B&C. From a former peak of $48 to $50 a week, wages slipped to a range of $38 to $40.

Anti-Ward Baking Company poster, **Bakers' Journal and Deutsche-Amerikanische Baeckerzeitung,** *June 2, 1923.*

The Chicago strike also acted as a crack in the dike of relations with the Ward Company. In April 1922, Ward refused to renew its agreement with Newark Local 84, the one local outside Chicago that was not under the national agreement. Then, in May 1923, it abandoned the national agreement covering the remainder of its plants, precipitating a nationwide strike involving locals in New York, Brooklyn, Boston, Providence, Philadelphia, Baltimore, Pittsburgh and Cleveland.

In Pittsburgh, Ward influenced the entire wholesale end of the industry to follow suit in the contest with the union and brought strikebreakers in from New York, continuing its operations with the help of police arrests of pickets. While Local 12's attorney looked after jailed members, the local organized members' wives and children into anti-Ward clubs to visit consumers in their neighborhoods and to pressure grocery store owners and businessmen not to handle Ward's bakery products. Through the efforts of B&C and American Federation of Labor organizers, communities throughout the mining districts of Western Pennsylvania returned carloads of non-union bread to Pittsburgh. By December, only 45 of Local 12's 400 strikers had not found other jobs.

These efforts encouraged Newark Local 84 to intensify its own anti-trust activities. With the aid of the Essex Trades Council and a representative of the AFL, it engaged in massive distribution of boycott materials and extensive pressuring of local businesses. By August, it was reporting that Ward had lost some 70 percent of its trade in the country and seashore communities of New Jersey.

None of these activities, however, was likely to soften the resolve of William Ward, who was about to initiate an unprecedented effort to consolidate the industry under his control. As late as May 1922, the *Bakers' Journal* had treated the challenge of the Trust with a certain innocence, carrying an article by G. Miller entitled "The Bakery Industry is Trustproof." According to Miller, the Trust could never provide the distinctive varieties of bakery products demanded by the foreign "colonies" of the large cities, nor operate with cost effectiveness in the country districts and small cities. The small baker, Miller argued, would survive as well because of the large demand for pies, cakes and confections which the Bread Trust could not satisfy. This is why, he observed, the Shults Baking Company and other large firms in the New York City area had lost ground in the previous three or four years.

By the middle of the decade, however, those who had accepted this line of thinking must have been hedging their bets in the face of a series of dramatic developments that were consolidating the industry. During 1922, Ward launched the United Bakeries Corporation, a holding company that acquired such large operations as Campbell Baking Company of Kansas City, and Shults of New York; in 1923, United Bakeries took over the 17-plant Ward Baking Company of New York, owned by Ward's uncle. In 1924, Ward organized the Continental Baking Corporation of Maryland, capitalized at $200 million, which acquired the United Bakeries, the American Bakery Company of St. Louis, and a host of others.

By 1926, Continental controlled 91 plants in the United States and nine in Canada. Meanwhile, in 1925, Ward played a major role in establishing a separate venture, the General Baking Corporation of Maryland, which acquired the General Baking Company's 33-bakery operation and undertook a major expansion of its holdings. This paved the way for chartering Ward Food Products Corporation in January 1926 to bring under one roof all the properties of Continental, Ward and General, an empire controlling about 20 percent of the bread production of the United States.

In 1926, the Justice Department broke up this combine. In a consent decree following proceedings under the Sherman Anti-trust Act, the conglomerate dissolved into three independent corporations. They were free, however, to continue acquiring independent companies in competition with one another.

This unprecedented capitalization of the industry was matched by the enormous expansion of chain store baking in the 1920s. The Great Atlantic & Pacific Tea Company set the trend. In 1920, it owned two bakeries; by 1930, 35. In 1921, its Chicago plant had joined with the Chicago Bakers' Club in adopting the open shop, and in the twenties A&P earned the reputation as "particularly unfriendly" to organized labor. When the chain began to ship bread from its plant in Buffalo to its 60 stores in Rochester in 1924, Local 14 rightly regarded it as "an invasion."

A&P and other chains enjoyed substantial cost savings through the control of the retail outlets for their product and generally undersold other brands by one to three cents per loaf. What is more, they regularly advertised their bread at a retail price below what other grocers had to pay for bread produced by wholesalers, even if it meant that the chains had to sell the bread at less than their cost of production. They were using bread as one of several select items to lure prospective customers from neighborhood grocery stores. By 1927, Ward was countering A&P's 14,000-store operation and other chain competition by including a coupon worth five cents with each loaf of bread. Joe Schmidt, organizing in Cleveland in 1927 for the B&C, wondered what would be left of the trade after this "fight for supremacy" among the giants.

Local autonomy limited the B&C's response to the grocery chains. as it had in the open shop campaign of Ward Baking Company. The Massachusetts State Board in 1924 developed the so-called "Massachusetts Plan" that would have united locals in presenting their demands to the national management of any chain grocery. This approach, the Board argued, would counteract the familiar situation in which a "self-important" individual store manager refused to do business with a local union. It would also prevent chains from signing contracts in some cities while singling out other localities for the open shop.

In cooperation with the Connecticut State Board, the Massachusetts Board tried to sell the idea to locals in the New England area. "To our surprise," it reported, "we met with the greatest opposition from the strongest locals from which we had expected the greatest cooperation." In April, the General Executive Board considered the plan and concluded that the constitution guaranteed "full autonomy" to the locals, that each local had "the exclusive right to declare when they shall or shall not strike," and that it would be "a dangerous proposition to bind all local unions to an iron-clad policy of the nature presented." The International, it decided, was limited to deciding whether or not a given strike deserved its sanction and support.

National membership figures during the decade proved fairly stable, considering the general open shop climate. The number of members in good standing peaked in 1921 at 28,070. Postwar depression and concerted action by employers registered the following year in a steep decline to 24,165. Thereafter the figure settled at about 22,000.

This decline caused the B&C to consolidate its operations to some extent. In January 1918, during the heady war years, the members had voted to levy an assessment of $1 a year for three years in order to accumulate funds for establishing an old age pension. When this proved unrealistic, the members voted to terminate the program and use the funds toward paying for a new national headquarters building. The headquarters, at 2719 North Wilton Avenue on Chicago's North Side, opened in 1922. The B&C paid the $79,418.48 cost outright, with more than half coming from the pension funds.

In addition to abandoning the pension, the B&C voted at its 18th convention in Los Angeles in September 1923 not to fill a vacancy resulting from Charles Iffland's illness. In October, Iffland went to the Montrose Avenue Hospital in Chicago suffering from what was described as intestinal complications. When he died on October 13, an era passed with him. Each of the remaining officers—Myrup, Hohmann and Koch—had immigrated as teenagers and first joined the B&C around the time of the Spanish-American War in the late 1890s. Iffland was the last officer tied to the founding of the Union itself. In the light of the difficult times, the 1923 convention realigned the remaining three officers to take up the slack. Hohmann became corresponding and recording secretary, retaining responsibility for the *Bakers' Journal*. Koch remained financial secretary, and Myrup became secretary-treasurer. The convention also reduced the number of organizers from five to three.

After sustaining one of its heaviest periods of strike activity in the early 1920s, the B&C attempted at mid-decade to hold the line as much as possible without members walking off the job. The

91

General Executive Board's annual session in early 1926 decided that in the area of strikes, it had left too much to local autonomy, often with "disastrous" results. In the future it would insist on giving much greater consideration to the possibility of success before sanctioning an action that would draw on the International's resources. What is more, it provided that the International representative it assigned to investigate each contemplated strike action should have the power to require the local involved to conduct its strike vote by secret, rather than open, ballot.

The Board modified the standard features of the contracts themselves. All new contracts would have to contain a clause continuing them in full force until the signing of a new agreement, the Board explaining that "while an agreement is still in force, a much better understanding can be reached and facilitated. . . ." No local thereafter could cancel its agreement without Board sanction. Furthermore, the Board strongly recommended that locals, wherever possible, sign multi-year agreements.

Faced with serious constraints in the 1920s, the B&C presented a fragmented image. Through most of the decade it made no headway with Ward and little with Continental and General, though a few locals maintained contractual relations with the latter two. While A&P stonewalled the Union, the National Tea Company stores marketed union labeled bread, and many chains fell somewhere between. In 1928, St. Louis Local 4 demonstrated that a strong local could bring even the large recalcitrants to terms. Both Ward and A&P opened new modern plants there, and both signed with the local early in the year. Jack Zamford, addressing the Chicago Union Label League in the fall, took heart from these developments. They showed, he observed, that "large corporations are not built on sentiment." A delegate from the electrotypers union who had been in touch with the A&P management agreed that A&P's main concern was profits; "it will deal with organized workers when it proves profitable."

Outside of the Trust, the picture was equally disjointed. The *Bakers' Journal* in 1921 listed Baltimore, Buffalo, Dayton, Detroit, Indianapolis, Minneapolis, New York, Philadelphia, St. Paul and Toledo as cities where the large shops remained unorganized despite efforts by the Union. In New York City, the independent bakers' unions, now in their second decade, organized into the Amalgamated Food Workers and continued to compete actively with the B&C locals of the city. Only the Jewish locals in the city, International officials told the delegates to the 1923 convention, had escaped the effects of the division; particularly in the larger shops, conditions were becoming "worse and more intolerable every year." Intermittant merger talks throughout the decade were unable to close this breach.

Jewish locals also proved the exception in Boston, where B&C Organizer Chris Kerker reported at the end of the decade that the wage scale was "below that of any other city I know of...." Jewish bakeries there, he claimed, paid almost twice the wages of what he called the "American" bakeries, despite charging no more for their bread. In Chicago, Jack Zamford noted that the Jewish bakeries organized by Local 237 were enjoying the highest wages and best working conditions and were the "aristocrats" of the trade. German Local 2, on the other hand, was contending with the introduction of machinery as well as the "hard knocks" of the open shop campaign.

Even in Los Angeles which, after the open shop campaigns, continued to enjoy the reputation as a "scab town" into the 1930's, the tight organization of bakeries in the Jewish ghetto was the exception. Jewish Local 453 there confronted a synchronized attempt by the Merchants and Manufacturers' Association in May 1926 to place non-union men in the bakeries. When the union refused to work with these men, the owners locked out its members. Despite police arrests of union pickets, the general population of the neighborhood rallied to the union's side. Wives of the bakers carried on a house-to-house label crusade. Six of the 16 bakeries signed quickly, and they worked around the clock for the rest of the strike producing union-made bread. The local supplemented this production by starting a cooperative plant. Members of Local 453, meanwhile, worked turns in the unionized plants, sharing the work until they successfully signed a contract with their employers in early June.

St. Louis Local 4 thrived in the 1920's, a report in 1924 placing it at 1,200 members and in "splendid financial condition." Denver Local 26 culminated a decade of successful organizing among the larger bread firms by signing a contract in 1928 with its longtime nemisis, the Old Homestead Bakery. The Homestead, having by this time suffered a loss of about two-thirds of its business, according to Local 26 Business Agent Ray Lowderback, finally came under the ownership of "a real man" who signed with the union.

At the same time, however, Joseph Schmidt found Milwaukee struggling with a seven-day work-week and top wages of $20 to $25 a week; "years will be required," Schmidt thought, "in order to drag the bakery workers of Milwaukee out of the mire of deplorable industrial conditions...." In Detroit, Schmidt visited one of the city's large shops in 1928 along with an organizer from Polish Local 77. The shop superintendant informed him that Detroit was an open-shop town. Schmidt observed that the "arrogance and contempt" of the large chain store shops in Detroit paralleled the notorious suppression of organization in the automobile industry.

At different points in the decade, the B&C identified large areas of the country where it had made no meaningful penetration. In 1921, in the industrial heartland area stretching from Altoona, Pa., to Cleveland and from Wheeling, W. Va., to Erie, Pa., a 200-mile by 150-mile rectangle, the Union seemed unable to make serious inroads outside the major cities. In the great number of small towns in this area, B&C locals were of the weak "sunflower" variety, and a baker was more likely to secure employment there through supply houses and yeast agents than through their union.

Charles Hohmann, addressing the Wisconsin State Federation of Labor's annual convention in July 1928, complained that only 189 bakery workers had joined the B&C statewide. There were a few dozen in each of six cities, 30 in all of Milwaukee, and none in such cities as Racine, Green Bay, Sheboygan, La Crosse, Eau Claire, Janesville, Manitowoc, Marinetta, Stevens Point, Waukesha, Merrill, Rhinelander, Wisconsin Rapids, Portage, Menomenie, Monroe and Sturgeon Bay. In Texas at about the same time there were no locals in Houston, Beaumont, Austin and Waco. Where locals existed—as in Dallas, Fort Worth, San Antonio, Wichita Falls and Amarillo—they were struggling.

Not only was the picture very uneven geographically, but within the overall structure of the industries it represented, the B&C made little progress among certain kinds of workers. It had, for instance, organized some candy workers before the turn of the century and as early as 1903 reported nine locals of candy makers totalling about 500 workers. This, however, was in a portion of the industry employing about 20,000 workers, with 19 factories operating under the National Candy Company alone.

At the beginning of World War I, New York, Massachusetts and Pennsylvania were the largest candy producers in the country. Alma Wismer, an investigator from the Women's Trade Union League of Boston, found that the ordinary candy worker in Massachusetts was a woman under 25 years of age, living at home, and earning under $6 a week. Most were American-born, though many were clearly identifiable as of Italian, Irish, Jewish and Syrian extraction. Men made the fillings for the candy, but once the hardened fillings reached the dipping room, candy making was women's work. In Boston, Wismer found, the older skilled dippers, the "backbone" of the industry, were for the most part Italian women who spoke little English; "their men folks do not permit them to attend meetings, or they have home to see to after work." Compounding the difficulty of organizing the women was the seasonality of the work. From September to Christmas time, the women worked 54 hours a week. The factories closed for ten days to two weeks after Christmas, and then began running from three to five days a week depending on orders. After a two-week closing in July, the industry began gearing up for its busy season once again.

Under these circumstances, organization in the candy industry, proved fleeting. The Boston workers organized and struck the Apollo candy factory on the North End in 1913. They won reduced hours and increased pay, advances that quickly spread to other factories in the area. Then the local dissolved. "Girls enter and leave the candy business weekly," Wismer explained. "They go into other work, they marry, they leave the city." Three years after the strike, she estimated, only one fifth of the women who had struck in 1913 were still working in the industry.

During the wartime labor shortage, some candy workers became militant for a time and achieved substantial improvements. Seattle Local 156, with men organized in its main body and women in an auxiliary, secured better conditions from the "Kandy Kaisers" and major cracker companies. Strong locals functioned for a time in San Francisco and Peoria, while St. Louis Local 4 tried to steer candy and cracker workers away from the practice of spontaneous strikes and toward developing a stable and permanent organization. A successful strike in Chicago for a time achieved an eight-hour day, 44-hour week.

Wages rose during the war, but in other ways conditions resembled those before the war. Women who had earned $28 a week in gas mask factories returned to dipping in New York City for $9 a week. In Philadelphia, according to a report by the United States Department of Labor, women earned $9.60 a week in the busy season, a 40 percent increase over 1915. Men, on the other hand, earned $18.35 in the same season, a 75 percent increase. In the slow season, almost 50 percent of the women lost their jobs, only 3.4 percent of the men.

At the same time, the impulse to organize disintegrated. A report at the 1920 B&C convention summarized that "so far there has been no desire on the part of the men and women employed in the candy industry to warrant extensive organizing work." When E.J. Brach reduced wages in 1921, it had no union to contend with. "The candy workers of Chicago were organized several times and we have tried our utmost to maintain a local," the Bakers' Journal offered, "but as soon as conditions were gained they went back to work, forgetting the organization."

Throughout the decade, candy making, along with cracker baking and ice cream making, remained the poorest organized segments of the B&C's constituency; the latter was rapidly completing a transition from a bake shop trade to an assembly line process in large dairies. Delegates to the B&C's convention in Los Angeles in August 1926, decided that these, as well as the manufacturing end of the bread industry, might be easier to organize if the locals did not insist on bargaining for the same wages and working conditions for unskilled workers in modern machine plants as enjoyed by skilled workers in hand shops. They advised locals to devise separate agreements for hand shops and machine shops.

In general, the B&C had no ready answers for the lull of the 1920s. The General Executive Board touted the conservative demeanor by which, in the three years between the 1923 and 1926 conventions, locals had avoided strikes, "even to the extent, in numerous cases, of granting employers unjustified concessions from the original demands." William Schnitzler, who began his career as a baker in Newark, New Jersey, in 1924 and rose to become B&C president in 1950 (and later secretary-treasurer of the national AFL-CIO), remembered later in retirement that in the 1920s "there were never any international problems, only local members. . . ." General officers tended to stay at headquarters in Chicago. Locals relied on local coalitions to strengthen their hands with their employers, appealing to unions in the central labor bodies of their cities who could bring pressure on bakeries through their preference for union-labeled bread.

Often, as well, locals cooperated with bread salesmen in the Teamsters union who worked for the same employers. The relationship between bakers and bakery salesmen had been a complex one, evolving from a time when the bakers delivered bread by horse and wagon after finishing the work in the shop. Gradually the Teamsters union asserted jurisdiction over the drivers, supported by the AFL's principle that there should be only one union per trade. The same logic that gained the B&C an AFL endorsement of its jurisdiction over bakers in hotels and restaurants cost the Union the Federation's support in the case of the drivers. Resolution No. 43 of the AFL's 1911 convention instructed the B&C to turn over to the Teamsters all drivers who were currently in the bakers' organization. The B&C never acceded to the demand. Nevertheless, over the following years, the Teamsters succeeded in "weaning away" the drivers, as the B&C General Executive Board explained to the 1936 convention, through the "pressure of their local economic power and tempting offers."

Over the years, however, local bakers and teamsters unions found that failure to coordinate their negotiations with employers could result in defeat for both of them. In Chicago, the lesson had been a bitter one. In 1910, bakery salesmen "stuck to their wagons" during the bakers' strike. In the 1919 strike, the bakers agreed to pay the teamsters' members benefits of $12 a week to keep them off the job; the bakers paid out $29,000 in such benefits before exhausting their treasury, after which the salesmen returned to work. During the 1921 bakers' strike, Teamsters' President Daniel Tobin personally intervened to warn his Chicago members that they could expect no financial support if they went out on a sympathy strike. He counseled that in such hard times, the bakers should follow the teamsters' example and submit to wage cuts through arbitration. By comparison, a town like Pullman, Oregon, typified the many communities where the two organizations developed effective local working agreements to help them through this difficult decade, a correspondent reporting in 1923 that the two locals were "closely associated" and their interests "related intimately."

From a later period, the 1920s would seem in some ways to have been a period of idyllic calm before the storm. On July 20, 1929, Local 145 in Peoria held its annual picnic. The bread bakers "beat the dough" out of the cake bakers in the ball game, the local reported, and the families ran through a seemingly endless round of games, a tug-of-war, three-legged race, nail-driving contest, cracker eating contest, a race to finish a bottle of soda through a nipple, a watermelon eating contest, and one to catch a chicken, a gumdrop chewing contest and a fat man's race.

The euphoria of the afternoon belied the fact that an era was ending. In February, William Ward, the most powerful individual in the baking industry, died of heart disease at his desk in New York. Already, some troubling trends in the economy were affecting the industry he had dominated for almost two decades. Industrial production at the beginning of 1929 was running 16 percent higher than the same period six years earlier, and 8.4 percent higher than 1928. Accompanying this, however, was a decrease in employment. Some 30,000 fewer people worked in the industry in 1927 than in 1925. What is more, the remaining workers were sharing only 12 percent of the value of increased productivity. "How can the additional commodities be consumed," the *Bakers' Journal* asked in April 1929, "when the purchasing power is destroyed?" Six months later, investors asked the same question, abandoning American industry in a panic that ushered in the Great Depression.

Some locals were more poorly prepared than others to weather the Depression. In Philadelphia, the industry was in a shambles more than a year before the great stock market crash. In the summer of 1928, Organizer Chris Kerker reported that unemployment in the industry was so bad that bakers were willing to work just for room and board. At Freihofer's and Kolb's, workers suffered deplorable conditions in silence for fear of losing their jobs if they complained. Employment agencies, Kerker noted, were already "loaded to capacity with people hunting vainly for jobs."

Thirty-six other bakery locals at that time had unemployment systems in place that helped them to absorb the Depression's first shocks. While a handful of these programs predated World War I, Buffalo Local 16's having begun in 1887, most were a product of the 1920s. Typically, they combined one or more of three kinds of assistance. Direct unemployment benefit payments were usually available only during the coldest months. Members of Seattle Local 9 were eligible for $7.50 per week for any period of unemployment between October 1 and May 1. San Francisco Local 24 provided $10 a week between December and March. In addition, locals often operated employment bureaus from which employers usually agreed to hire all their help. Seattle Local 9 was placing 60 members a year in jobs through its bureau. Spokane Local 74, with just over 200 members, reported receiving 150 applications for steady employees in 1927 and another 1,200 applications for short time help. Some locals operated a time sharing plan popularized by Jewish locals, working members giving up one or two days a week as the situation required. A provision of the union contract with the employer generally required the employer to accept jobbers the union sent as substitutes for regular workers. In August 1928, Washington, D.C., Local 118 reported that half its members were working only five days a week under this arrangement. The one day a week that members of Baltimore Local 209 were giving up at the same time was enough to furnish unemployed members with two to four days of work a week. New York City Local 500, in describing its work-sharing program, suggested that the full week was "almost wholly a thing of the past."

By the time of the B&C's 20th convention at St. Louis in September 1929, the General Executive Board was warning that the "ruthless displacement of labor" had attained "dangerously growing proportions...." Unemployment, however, was only the beginning of a chain of problems that faced the Union during the Depression. The Depression intensified price competition between bakeries. In Niagara Falls, New York, competition among brands in the spring of 1931 forced prices down to two cents a loaf and drove

The Bakers widely distributed promotional fans in the 1930s, advertising the union label.

some owners to desperation. At one bakery, two gunman forced five workers to line up against a wall and then poured kerosene into the fresh dough. Before departing, they warned the employees that if the bakery did not stop operation, they would blow it up. In Buffalo early in 1932, a large non-union bakery was selling its loaves for four cents and allowing each purchaser to purchase 15 rolls for an additional cent. Initiatives of this sort put union-organized firms under tremendous pressure.

Generally, non-union firms were able most quickly to take advantage of the growing availability of cheap unemployed labor to enforce wage cuts on their workers. Henry Alvino's experience was typical. He had started as a hand greaser at A&P in Pittsburgh in 1926, working his way up to the molder machine and the divider and moving to a subsidiary of Ward in 1929. When the Depression came, his wages dropped from $25 a week to $13.20 while his hours went up from 48 to 80. Curtis Sims started work at American Bakeries in Chattanooga in 1927, where beginners earned from $16 to $18 a week for 48 to 50 hours of work. When the Depression came, wages dipped to a dollar a day, hours were "until the work was done," and the week was seven days long. Wage cuts of this sort gave non-union shops a competitive advantage and sustained the epidemic of price cuts that forced union firms to respond in kind.

Caught in the spiral of price and wage cuts, locals reacted in different ways. Local 184 in Little Rock and Hot Springs, Arkansas, found it difficult to overcome the "prevailing apathy" of members toward the union; its employers enjoyed a virtual moratorium on the enforcement of the working conditions in their contract. Other locals, however, sought to fight their way out by exercising their leverage with consumers. In some places, they inaugurated buy-at-home campaigns to embargo shipments from out-of-town non-union shops. Washington Local 118 joined with Bakery Salesmen's Local 33 of the Teamsters to challenge the importation of loaves by A&P which at five cents were priced lower than cost. They bought time on the radio airwaves following Amos 'n Andy broadcasts, sent thousands of communications to workers' homes, and made special appeals to the Federal Employees' Union. Their effort gained the support of the Washington Merchants and Manufacturers' Association, the Federation of Women's Clubs of Washington, the Washington Chamber of Commerce, the Citizens Association and the Housekeepers' Alliance. Hamilton, Ohio, had a similar campaign.

Where a local was especially strong, as in Denver, it was able to strike to maintain wages. In a four-hour walk-out at five major bakeries in 1932, the first bakers' union strike there since 1917, Local 26 turned back a 20-percent reduction. Vancouver union bakeries held the line on wages, despite cuts by every non-union bakery in the city, by launching an intensive label campaign complete with an extensive display of union cards at bakeries and grocery stores, to sustain their employers' business.

Chicago locals that had for years all but ignored the fast growing South Side, inaugurated a major campaign in late 1928 to organize what they estimated were 650 bakeries between the Loop and the Indiana border. Jack Zamford set up operations on West 69th Street and Locals 2, 13, 49, 62, and 237 pumped in 25 cents per member per month to challenge the 12- to 14-hour day and other non-union conditions flourishing in that sector of town. This operation continued for years; the 1932 phase concentrated on 63rd Street, where union representatives found several bosses trying to work their shops alone or with a single helper rather than the three- to four-man force the work required. Confident of success because of the overwhelmingly

MASS MEETING
for all Bakers of the South Side

Saturday, December 8th, 1928, 7:30 P.M. at Normal Hall, 6908 S. Halsted St.

Why must you work long hours for little pay?

Your are helpless unless you join the Bakers' Union!

Your boss belongs to his organization. Why should you not belong to yours?

Wake Up Bakery Workers on the South Side!

Come to this meeting and bring your fellow workers along!

GOOD SPEAKERS

The Bakers' Joint Executive Board of Chicago

649 W. 69th Street   Englewood 2835

Mass meeting call during Chicago South Side campaign, Bakers' Journal and Deutsche-Amerikanische Baeckerzeitung, *Dec. 8, 1928.*

working-class character of the neighborhood, the bakers campaigned with the determined slogan, "63rd Street Must Be Organized Even If We Have To Fight Our Way Through."

Taking readings on the overall impact of the Depression on the B&C, Joe Schmidt was still able to generate optimism two or three years after the panic. In February 1931, for instance, he noted that the B&C had suffered little shrinkage in membership—thanks, he surmised, to the International's benefit system and the unemployment benefits of many locals. The following January, he observed that, in contract negotiations, most locals had "emerged unscathed;" there had been wage reductions, but "the loss would have been far greater had there been no restriction of organized resistance on the part of our members." Union employers had not only proven willing to hold the line against wage cuts for as long as possible, but had in many instances cooperated with the Union in spreading the work through shorter work weeks and lay-offs in rotation.

Still, by 1932, locals all along the line began to wear thin. At the March 1932 General Executive Board meeting, Schmidt admitted that locals could only resist wage reductions to a certain point without endangering the Union itself. "Local environments" in the last analysis determined wages, he declared, and "ninety-eight percent" of past wage reductions were the result of price reductions by non-union concerns "gradually dragging in the union concerns." In any case, according to Board member Pete Beisel, unemployment, rather than wage reductions, was the greatest problem facing the Union, since all the large locals that had unemployment benefits had now depleted their treasuries. After listening to a report by Andy Myrup on the potential bankruptcy of locals, the Board recommended that locals discontinue unemployment benefits and rely instead on work-sharing arrangments in cooperation with employers. Wherever unemployment benefits continued, the Board suggested that recipients who were able-bodied should be required to engage in compensatory agitational work for the Union, not only for its own sake but also because of the "demoralizing effect upon our membership" of unrestricted handouts. In addition, the Board emphasized that cash payments for unemployment or relief should come from special funds for that purpose and not from the working revenue of the locals.

While these administrative principles were of utility in protecting the basic structure of the organization, they could not begin to confront the large problem: the Union's resources were finite, and the needs seemed to have no end. William McGuern, Board member, business representative of Seattle Local 9, and president of the Seattle Central Labor Council, submitted detailed figures on the in-

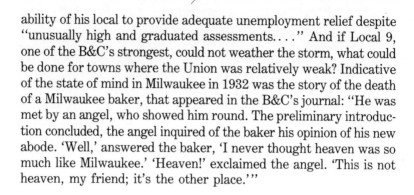

ability of his local to provide adequate unemployment relief despite "unusually high and graduated assessments...." And if Local 9, one of the B&C's strongest, could not weather the storm, what could be done for towns where the Union was relatively weak? Indicative of the state of mind in Milwaukee in 1932 was the story of the death of a Milwaukee baker, that appeared in the B&C's journal: "He was met by an angel, who showed him round. The preliminary introduction concluded, the angel inquired of the baker his opinion of his new abode. 'Well,' answered the baker, 'I never thought heaven was so much like Milwaukee.' 'Heaven!' exclaimed the angel. 'This is not heaven, my friend; it's the other place.'"

The advances of the B&C and other unions under the New Deal came at a time of heightened awareness of the restrictions on liberty under Hitler in Germany and Mussolini in Italy.

6

Depression and Recovery

*"That system's wrong that hoards the surplus
wheat. While hungry children daily cry for bread."*

(From a poem in the Bakers' Journal, 1932.)

wo generations of leaders brought the B&C through the period of the Great Depression and the Great War. For the old guard occupying the national positions as officers, board and quorum members, and full-time organizers this was a heroic end to a proud endeavor, and they strove for all they were worth to see it through and see it continue. Yet in a sense, both time and events had caught up with them; their attrition rate was frightful and no doubt in some cases related to the crises they were forced to withstand. At the same time, a younger generation of local leaders, brought into their positions by the wave of the Depression, juxtiposed a new, tough, militant, and impatient style upon the more conservative demeanor the B&C carried with it from the 1920s.

While administratively cautious and conservative, the B&C had never abandoned its more radical political agenda. Sound business management was a matter of survival and effectiveness. It did not alter the basic commitment of the Union to establishing a labor party independent of the capitalists for whom its members worked. Consistently over the years, B&C leaders had criticized Samuel Gompers for what they thought of as his collaboration with business leaders in the National Civic Federation and his politics of "begging favors" from established parties dominated by the business class. At the B&C's 18th convention in 1923, Joseph Schmidt, on behalf of the committee on resolutions, successfully moved that B&C delegates to the American Federation of Labor convention seek to alter the

Federation's constitution and by-laws to "encourage a distinct working class political party. . . composed of and organized by the American Federation of Labor. . . with the assistance of farmers and other organizations, progressive clubs, and individuals or groups. . . ." By the end of the decade, the *Bakers' Journal* masthead had for more than 20 years carried the Socialist credo, "the emancipation of the working class must be accomplished by the working class itself." Now, overnight, the Bakers' leaders were thrown into national political life as part of the cast of a recovery program orchestrated by the Democratic party.

The B&C canceled its scheduled convention in 1933, and its national leaders set up a Washington bureau. With economic counsel, they prepared to participate in Franklin Roosevelt's New Deal. The National Industrial Recovery Act called for establishing a code in each industry to regulate competitive practices and working conditions. This meant that the B&C had to draw up briefs and provide testimony at hearings designed to establish separate codes for the baking, biscuit and cracker, pretzel, confectionery, macaroni, and cocoa and chocolate industries. Its leaders quickly perceived, however, how little leverage these forums provided.

The process of code-making proved frustrating. Myrup, Hohmann, and Koch, along with Jacob Goldstone, Jack Zamford and Joseph Schmidt, testified in the baking industry hearings in January 1934, arguing for the adoption of a 35-hour week for machine shops, 38 for handcraft shops, and restoration of wage levels to those of July 1929. On the other side, employer spokesmen bent every effort to promote their version of industry standards. In one case that B. H. Walker, secretary of San Diego Local 90, reported, the manager of the Continental Baking Company in his town called his workers together and handed them the master bakers' code proposal, asking them to sign it. Fearing the loss of their jobs, they all signed; the manager forwarded the document to Washington to support corporate proposals at the code hearings.

Eventually, the employers had things mostly their own way. The code that President Roosevelt signed in May 1934 adopted a 40-hour week for machine shops, 48 for handicraft bakeries, and a minimum wage of forty cents per hour, with the exception of icers, wrappers, and cleaners who could be employed at 80 percent of the minimum. Despite strong Union opposition, the code included a Southern differential of five cents per hour below the minimum, "a partial recognition," according to National Recovery Administrator Hugh Johnson, "of a substantially larger differential heretofore existing and of certain other factors peculiar to the South where home baking is a more competitive factor and per capita consumption much lower." The code did provide, however, that women should receive the same rates as men in operations where male and female employees customarily performed the same work.

Other industry hearings proved no more satisfying. The biscuit and cracker hearings actually stalled through 1934 and into 1935. Meanwhile the confectionery industry code adopted a 40-hour week, except during peak seasonal periods, which could amount to as much as 18 weeks a year. It established a minimum wage that varied not only sectionally but also according to population density and sex. Male workers' minimum ranged from 40 cents an hour in cities over 500,000 in population to 35 cents in areas under 100,000; women from 35 to 30 cents. A five-cent differential applied to the South.

Section 7(a) of the NIRA, which provided the basis for including working conditions in the codes, also guaranteed the right of employees to organize and bargain through representatives of their own choosing. Employers could not require their employees to join a company union or to refrain from joining another labor organization as a condition of employment. Throughout the early 1930s, however, B&C leaders warned members that these features of the NIRA would only be as effective a remedy as their own efforts made them.

Intimidation abounded. Nothing in the law, for instance, prevented employers from continuing to offer the company union as an option to workers, and even encouraging them to join. Corporations, the B&C warned, had put their lawyers to work to "trot out the company union in a new form." In Pittsburgh, according to one local bakers' official, managers in the large shops assembled their workers and assured them that they were going to receive all the benefits that were coming to them from the NIRA, and that they would get all these benefits by belonging to the company union. One of these spokesmen admitted that the companies could not fire an employee for joining another union, but he pointed out that "he could discharge them for not putting their hat on straight." The companies made the message even clearer, according to a local union official, by introducing a "veritable spy system" in all their shops.

These early experiences convinced the B&C leaders that the Union would not gain any respect it didn't earn; ". . . the community as a whole won't bestir itself," they warned, "until those directly interested—that is THE WORKERS—bestir themselves and FIGHT FOR ENFORCEMENT." The key opportunity of the NIRA was the potential it offered to reach previously unorganized workers. "If there are no big and STRONG unions in any industry," the *Bakers' Journal* cautioned in July 1933, "there will be no benefits. . . ." The real battle, therefore, was the battle for members. A new line in the masthead beginning with the July 15th issue of the journal entreated, "Double the Membership under NIRA!" The International called on bakers in the name of patriotic duty as well as economic responsibility to "ORGANIZE TO COOPERATE WITH THE PRESIDENT, so that industry may serve humanity and that no man shall starve."

During the next decade and a half, the B&C experienced the most remarkable period of growth in its history. Encouraged by the International, locals established special lower rates for initiation and for reobligating older members in arrears, and vastly expanded their rolls. Meanwhile, dozens of new locals materialized. Whereas the B&C had cancelled its scheduled convention in 1933, the year its membership rolls bottomed out at barely above the 16,000 mark, the convening of the 21st convention in Pittsburgh in 1936 took place in a triumphant atmosphere. The International had added more than 20,000 dues-paying members in three years; its membership now stood at 37,376.

The three years between 1933 and 1936 represented a sea change for the B&C in more than just numbers. Expansion brought with it a new group of rank-and-file leaders at the very time when the B&C was losing some of its longtime older troopers. B&C General Organizer Chris Kerker died suddenly in 1930. Despite suffering from a cold, the *Bakers' Journal* reported, he had taken charge of the "perpetual picketing" of Roseman's bakery for his Local 144 of Yonkers, N.Y. Though relatively young at 49 and a man of robust health and powerful physique, he experienced acute pains in his side after two days and nights with virtually no sleep. He died moments after his comrades got him to his home.

There followed Max Freund in 1932, the 67-year-old General Executive Board member, an immigrant from Prague who had been a member of the Union since 1886. In 1933, Gus Becker died at 63 of a heart ailment. A Board member from the West Coast, he had been active in the bakers' union in Germany before coming to New York City and, in the years before World War I, moving to Seattle and San Francisco. Then, in 1936, two of the three officers of the B&C succumbed within months of each other. An ailing Henry Koch stepped down as International financial secretary in March, Charles Hohmann taking his position while Joseph Schmidt became International corresponding and recording secretary and editor of the *Bakers' Journal*. In September, Hohmann collapsed of a paralytic stroke while on the platform at the 21st convention in Pittsburgh, dying at St. Francis Hospital shortly afterwards. Herman Winter, the president of Kansas City Local 218, who had served both as a Board member and as a general organizer, took Hohmann's place. Three months later, on December 28, 1936, Henry Koch died at the age of 59.

While these events represented more of a thinning of the old guard than a changing of the guard, developments on the local level were signalling the underlying generational change that was underway. Wesley Reedy's introduction to the bakery in the Philadelphia trade came at the height of the Depression. In 1931, newly married, out of work for months, "depressed, with a loss of inner dignity," as he would later recount, he managed to find work at Mee's Bakery through a tip from a close friend. The friend was leaving Mee's to take a job driving a coal truck. In those days, bakery jobs usually went to workers recommended by the route salemen who distributed the bakeries' products to the independent grocery stores. Reedy got the job simply by squatting in it, punching his friend's time card each day and collecting $18 in wages for 80 to 85 hours a week in an envelope marked with his friend's name.

After a few weeks, Reedy became aware that some of the older German bakers in the shop were members of B&C Local 6, which had hardly more than two dozen members at the time, scattered in several shops, none of them under contract. While the local's secretary was shop steward at Mee's, few would discuss the union in the shop; "in those years the mention of the word union, and that person was out of a job," Reedy explained. After work, however, the nearest beer saloon was full of talk about what the Nazi's were doing to the German unions and about what President Roosevelt's radio talks meant for the common man in America. "President Roosevelt at the time made many favorable comments. . .as well as I can recall it, that 'if I was a worker I would be a union man,'" Reedy remembered. "The whole idea of unionizing was in every plant, and every shop."

Reedy and a few other "neophytes" began the task of handbilling all the shops in the city, steered the union through partially successful short general strikes in 1933 and 1934, and then redoubled their efforts to sign up members in the city's major plants. In the spring of 1936, after they had signed up 80 percent of the workers at the major plants in the city, they achieved a major breakthrough at the three plants of the American Stores Bakeries, the company agreeing to union recognition, wage increases, several holidays, a one-week vacation, and seniority rights. Over the following four years, the local organized all the large firms with the exception of Tastee Cake.

Younger leaders like Reedy brought a new style to the B&C. At his first union meeting, he rose to request that the secretary read the minutes of the previous meeting in English; after some discussion, the members agreed. "It is a regrettable fact," Reedy reflected, "that the accent and speech of the International staff was not readily acceptable by the brash young American born membership."

Reedy and his cohorts grew impatient with the cautious and conservative approach of the International representatives who came into Philadelphia to advise them. "They'd sit down, talk about our problem, which somehow they never resolved. . . .We wanted action. We wanted it, not a month from now, we wanted it that night." The younger men even organized confectionery plants despite the advice of the International that it was as waste of their time because of the predominance of women workers and seasonal work. By 1937, candy workers' Local 350 was a thriving organization of 1,500 members and Local 439, representing the candy workers at Whitman's, had several hundred more.

Epitomizing the distance between the older and younger leaders was International Representative John Geiger. He came to the United States from Germany in 1893 and had been a member of Knights of Labor Local Assembly 2389 and B&C Local 118 in Washington, D.C., before rising to the General Executive Board in 1915. In the 1930s, he was, by Reedy's measure, an "old, old, old man." A mainstay and important contributor to the old B&C, he was out of his element among the newer activists. "No way could he take the long hours that we were working organizing," Reedy observed. "He just didn't understand our method of operation."

Other new leaders illustrated the same impatience. Curtis Sims, who led the surge of bakery organizing in the South beginning with his local in Chattanooga, chafed every time Board member Herman Schad, an old-line "Dutchman" from New Orleans, came to town. He also found the red tape of International rules frustrating— Andy Myrup's insistence, for instance, on following procedure on a range of practices from the incurring of expenses for organizing to the imposition of trusteeships. In Pittsburgh, where Sam Wehofer, an older German Socialist, had built up Local 12, Henry Alvino rose to became business agent on the strength of a growing membership of non-German members from machine shops. Within this local, Alvino joined in the movement to conduct and record meetings in English. He subsequently became an International organizer, resigning at one point, however, because Andy Myrup wanted him to take the bus rather than using an automobile to ride the organizing circuit.

These personal differences reflected more fundamental changes in the Union. As the International continued to expand, reaching 83,000 dues paying members by the time of the 1941 convention in St. Paul, its chemistry irreversibly altered. The characteristic member was no longer a skilled worker of German background, the preponderance of the new members coming from machine shops, most of them native American in background, many of them women. Workers that many skilled bakers had previously disdained as "shoemakers" now outnumbered them in the organization. While workers in the handicraft shops and some stragetic workers in the mechanized shops still enjoyed a bargaining power intrinsic to their skill, it was the mass base of the organization that provided bargaining strength for the growing majority.

In fact, the typical B&C member may more closely have resembled the newly organized pretzel twisters of central Pennsylvania than the baker out of the small shop tradition. Pretzels had enjoyed an increasing popularity with the growing consumption of beer after the repeal of prohibition. On July 4, 1933, shortly after the passage of the NIRA, pretzel workers in Reading inaugurated a virtual rebellion. "Mass picket lines marched upon the half dozen or more plants in the city," Business Agent Earl White of the Reading Trades Council reported. "In every instance it resulted in thousands of dough twisters and their friends crowding the streets in which the plant was located, and menacingly threatening to do countless things in the event that it opened without a settlement. . . ." The strikes achieved seven closed shop and six preferential shop agreements and galvanized workers in other pretzel centers such as Allentown and York, with equally successful results. Pretzel workers took their place in the B&C in such locals as Local 168 in Reading and Local 231 in York.

Where machine hands sought admittance to old-line locals, craft-oriented bakers sometimes resisted. Henry Alvino, for instance, recalled that because the Pittsburgh bakers did not take in the helpers in the early 1930s, the helpers took the jobs of striking bakers who were trying to organize at Wards. In 1933, when the Pittsburgh bakers finally won their first contract of the new era with Ward's, it applied to all the Ward workers, organized in one big bakers' local. Donald Fink, later a B&C representative, recalled a similar resistance in his local, Local 213 of Cincinnati. Here, however, the machine hands organized in a separate auxiliary that eventually outgrew the parent local. Even as late as the late 1940's, though, the elite held the auxiliary at arm's length in Cincinnati.

Skilled workers at Cushman-Purity in New York City embraced

111

industrial unionism in 1935. Members of Local 50, they initially tried to bargain separately with company officials. The company, however, informed the regional National Recovery Administration compliance board that the skilled bakers represented only 400 out of its 3,000 employees and that the company therefore was not required by law to deal with the local. At that point the local reorganized as a "vertical" union, taking in the large majority of the workers. Even at this, it had an enormous struggle on its hands. Company managers now denounced the union as a "radical, industrial organization" and fought it bitterly for two years. In the period between May 1935, when the Supreme Court declared the NIRA unconstitutional, and September 1935, when the National Labor Relations (Wagner) Act reenacted a set of basic federal protections for union activity, the company weeded out groups of male workers, laying them off and replacing them, the union complained, with lower-paid women, imported Mexicans and paroled convicts whom the company could threaten to return to prison "if they even thought of striking." Local 50 struggled with the company until August 1937 when it achieved a contract guaranteeing the union shop in all six Cushman-Purity plants.

Even locals that continued to represent the handicraft shops were permanently transformed by the Depression. Symbolic of the alteration was Chicago Local 62, Andy Myrup's own local and until the Depression known as an organization of highly skilled Scandinavian craftsmen specializing in the most expensive goods in the industry. Hjalmer Anderson, Local 62's business agent, explained in a radio broadcast in November 1928 that the union was "composed of skilled mechanics and we are careful in the admittance of new members." It was, however, also one of the hardest hit by the Depression. Its jurisdiction on Chicago's North and Northwest Sides drew its trade heavily from among building trade workers who suffered severely from unemployment. Joblessness among 62's members followed, and those still finding work were too frightened about losing their jobs to report violations of the local's rules, much less to protest wage cuts.

"'What is the use' was the slogan," Charles Ingelsson, local recording secretary in 1933, recalled; "the officials slumbered, if not dead...." Then the sweeping successes of the Chicago South Side organizing campaign electrified the local. It ousted "a couple of dead corpses," according to Ingelsson, and imported a "live wire" from the South Side. The transformation that took place over the course of the next decade involved lifting the spell of "smug self-contentation," Ingelsson suggested. By 1941, it had 350

112

members in 135 shops and had become "a real melting pot for Americanism."

The disruptions of the Depression and the opportunities of the New Deal had the power to bury old disagreements that had long divided bakers in some communities. Local 19 in Cleveland had been a powerful organization at the time of World War 1, a local of 650 members in 1919 that had most of the major shops in the city under contract. An unsuccessful strike that year, followed by a split in the union, left it nearly dormant from 1920 until 1933. Its activities in the subsequent decade, however, not only reestablished Local 19 as a major force in the city but raised the star of another of the new generation of leaders.

Harvey Friedman, born in Kiev about 1900, was part of the remnant of Local 19 that had limped through the 1920s. From 1933 on, however, he was the epitomy of the new leader, working "day and night" in all branches of the trade, stirring a whirlwind of activity that buried the old dissensions in the local. When he became business agent in the fall of 1933, the local had less than 100 members. A year later, it had more than 1,200. With the cooperation of the Cleveland Federation of Labor, he conducted a successful mass picketing campaign of A&P warehouses that persuaded the Teamsters to cease deliveries to the grocery chain, shutting down A&P's Cleveland stores and paving the way for their unionization in 1934.

At the same time, Friedman led Local 19 through a strike against the city's major bread firms in the summer of 1934 in cooperation with the bakery drivers' union. At the beginning of June, 650 bakers struck Spang, General, Ward, Star, Grennan, Laubs and Speck. On August 14 the local won a preferential agreement from these firms providing that "all members of the Bakers' Local No. 19, now employed by these companies, or those that may join in the future, shall remain so during the life of this agreement without interference or coercion on the part of the employer." Five years later the leading bakeries signed their first closed-shop agreement requiring them to hire all their workers through the union.

Meanwhile, Friedman assisted Local 197 in organizing the candy industry, helping guide a secret organizing campaign that culminated in strikes at Fanny Farmer and Becker Candy companies in 1933 and a two-month strike at Becker in 1934. The four major candy producers in Cleveland signed a contract with Local 197 in 1934. Friedman also pushed for the organization of pie companies. In the mid-1930s, pie bakery workers were earning from 32 to 40 cents an hour, with female workers as low as 20 cents. Hours were sometimes as long as 75 a week. In 1942, Local 19 negotiated an agreement with the pie bakeries similar to that in force in other baking establishments. Female pie machine workers received 55 cents an hour through this agreement. "It has always been my contention," Friedman insisted, "that the pie workers are not any different from the workers in cake shops or other shops of Local 19...."

Divisions among bakers in New York City also dissolved under the impact of the Depression. At the bakery industry code hearings in 1933, the B&C was embarrassed by the inability of the workers to present a united position. Three separate organizations testified— the B&C, the Amalgamated Food Workers and an Industrial Bakery Workers' Union apparently under Communist leadership. "To all who were in attendance during those hearings," the General Executive Board related at the B&C's 1936 convention, "it was apparent that the employers as well as the Code administration authorities held up to ridicule this divided situation...."

During 1934 and 1935, the International and the Amalgamated drew together amid frantic efforts by supporters of the Communist-led United Front Committee of New York to have the Amalgamated join its "unity front" instead. "Facing a growing sentiment for affiliation with our International Union," a B&C representative reported in early 1935, "the opposition element in the ranks of the Amalgamated locals is feverishly at work in creating discord and raising false issues among the membership, or resort to terroristic tactics of violence to interfere with orderly discussions...." Tensions reached a peak in January 1935, when Amalgamated Branch 3 of Brooklyn, the largest local in the organization, held an election on the question of joining the B&C. Ballots from the referendum apparently made it no further than the furnace of the Brooklyn Labor Lyceum. The branches of the Amalgamated, nevertheless, each voted by a large majority to return to the International. By March 1935, the merger was complete, ending a division that had lasted more than 21 years and adding about 3,000 members to the B&C's rolls.

While the 1930s forced enormous adjustments within and among existing locals, it also saw the creation of wholly new locals in plants previously untouched by organization. As of June 1941, the B&C had 344 locals in 46 states and Canada. On the one hand, 11 of these were over 50 years old, another 33 over 40 years, and 63 more over 25. On the other hand, 100 new locals had received their charters since the 1936 convention. While 62,581 members worked in bread, cake and pie shops, there were now 10,630 in the candy and confectionery branch, 8,568 in biscuits and crackers, and 1,159 in the macaroni and noodle industry.

Many NABISCO workers at first organized as so-called Federal Labor Unions affiliated directly with the AFL rather than the B&C. The "awakening" of these workers under the NIRA was, by and large, a product of their own intiative, driven by the opportunities of the New Deal and their response to employers' attempts to organize them into company unions. Some joined the B&C either on a full dues paying basis or on a temporary non-beneficiary basis. But, as the B&C General Executive Board explained to the 1936 convention, some of these new unions "could not and would not" embrace the International with its "chain of benefits...and correspondingly larger dues requirements." The Board therefore approved their direct affiliation with the AFL on a temporary basis.

The experience of these organizations in the late 1930s tended to alter their perspective and drew them into the B&C. Wes Reedy recalled the extensive help his local rendered during the 1935 strike of the Philadelphia and New York Federal Labor Unions. These independent organizations, he realized, were enjoying "the best of two worlds" as low dues unions that could depend on the B&C for support. Over the next several years, therefore, "there was a lot of heart to heart talks and pretty plain cussing and straightening out of priorities...." Both Federal Labor Unions transferred their membership to the B&C before the end of the decade.

New mass locals contributed their own leaders to the new generation that was moving up in the B&C's ranks. James Landriscina, for instance, born in Naples, Italy, in 1901, apprenticed at Nabisco in New York in 1921. He came up in an organization which began as a Federal Labor Union and affiliated with the B&C as Local 405. Another young leader, William Galvin, was the driving force in Local 405, serving as president and business agent prior to his tragic death in an airplane crash in 1947. Galvin and Landriscina launched a drive to organize the New York candy industry in the late 1930s. By this time, the B&C was taking note of Landriscina, as a "sincere, militant and agressive fighter." He emerged as the business manager of candy Local 452 and in the summer of 1939 mapped out an organizing campaign affecting 80 of the industry's open shop firms. In 1941, the B&C St. Paul convention decided to add four positions to the General Executive Board, two for the candy and confectionery industry and two for biscuits and crackers. Landriscina became one of the Board members for the candy and confectionery jurisdiction.

A measure of the effectiveness of the B&C during the 1930s was the failure of the Congress of Industrial Organizations to establish any more than a beachhead in the baking industry. At the American Federation of Labor's convention in November 1935, B&C delegates aligned with those who were supporting the industrial form of unionism for mass production industries, Andy Myrup joining John L. Lewis and others in signing the minority report on the subject. Yet the B&C would not join in the efforts of that minority the day after the convention to launch the Committee for Industrial Organization for the purpose of conducting organizing drives on an industry-wide basis.

The Committee did not officially become a dual movement until 1938 when, following the AFL's expulsion of the Committee's affiliated organizations, it reconstituted itself as the Congress of Industrial Organizations. Nevertheless, B&C officials considered it a separatist movement from the beginning and regarded their own history as proof of the destructiveness of secessionism. Often enough, thereafter, elements of the CIO probed and tested the strength and commitment of the B&C to its new industrial base. The same determination and aggressiveness that sustained the International's recent expansion proved more than a match for the CIO's latter-day challenge.

John DeConcini experienced the CIO shortly after hitching a ride out of Pennsylvania's coal country on a coal truck and finding work at Bond in Philadelphia, with the help of an uncle, in March 1937. Fresh from a stint in a Civilian Conservation Corps camp, he began work as a pan greaser and baker's helper. Three months later the plant manager called the workers together and asked them to sign cards for the CIO. DeConcini was one of about 20 who would not sign. In Philadelphia, Wes Reedy explained, the CIO's approach was to work through employers, offering to write contracts on very favorable terms to the company in exchange for getting a toehold in the plant. The B&C on the other hand had its base in the shops. "Wes was my first contact...he inspired me," DeConcini recalled. "No one from the CIO ever came around." By an agreement mediated by Mayor S. D. Wilson, the CIO agreed to cease organizing in the bakery plants if it did not win an election among the workers at Freihofer's and Ward's. After suffering defeat in the election, the CIO withdrew.

Although the CIO enjoyed unusual advantages in some areas, it was often not able to translate these directly into organizational successes. Daniel Conway, who began work during the Depression in a Los Angeles pie shop and became business agent of Local 37 in 1937, remembered that the CIO based its effort there around a core of Communists who had been expelled from Local 37. While they had the support of the Longshoremen who "had a habit of showing up with cargo hooks," they were unable to make any inroads in Los Angeles.

United Mine Workers District 50 was able to organize bakers in some of the eastern mining districts. On the other hand, in Pittsburgh, surrounded, as Henry Alvino pointed out, by "steel, iron and coal," the B&C was able to expand its presence, particularly into the previously unorganized candy and biscuit plants, by paying part of the salaries of three organizers who put on an effective campaign. They worked very closely with the Teamsters and stayed "one step ahead" of the CIO organizers until the latter finally pulled out.

In Detroit, a center where the CIO was a dominant force, a mine workers' son who had fought as a Progressive miner against John L. Lewis' leadership of the UMW now led an effective campaign to organize the baking industry for the B&C. The Progressive Miners' organization had lost its encounter with Lewis but James Cross emerged with a reputation as someone to watch. The Progressives sent him to Brookwood Labor College after which he found work at Farm Crest Bakeries in Detroit in 1934. There he participated in a sitdown strike, became president of B&C Local 20 in 1936, and a year later, when his local merged with Local 326, became an International representative at the age of 25.

Under assignment from the International office, Cross took on the brunt of the CIO offensive in Detroit. By March 1938, he had most of the major shops of Detroit under closed shop agreements. In 1940, Local 326 Business Agent Alwin Quast reported that Cross had negotiated a two-year agreement with Farm Crest that effectively banished the CIO from the largest bakery in Detroit. According to Quast, Local 326 had expelled several workers who were actively supporting the CIO and the terms of the agreement required the company to discharge them. Cross was soon working out of Chicago where in 1941 he became a member of the General Executive Board representing the cracker and biscuit industry.

While the B&C determined to ward off CIO raids on its membership "with all the powers at our command," it also resisted what it regarded as the conspiracy on the part of some employers to pit the two labor organizations against one another. Where the CIO succeeded in organizing a previously unorganized establishment, the International preferred to yield the territory for the moment. Such was the case in Hershey, Pennsylvania, where the B&C was in the process of organizing Local 464 in 1937. Then, according to the General Executive Board, the CIO stepped in and with "false and impossible promises" lured the Hershey candy workers away. "We have constantly refused to permit operators and management in our industry to use our unions in any triangle contest that would be detrimental to the workers themselves," the General Executive Board later explained to the membership.

That was only part of the story, however, as the situation in Hershey demonstrated. During 1937, Hershey launched a campaign against the CIO with help from citizens' committees in the company-dominated community. The CIO local quickly faltered, and the company then attempted to introduce a company union. When the National Labor Relations Board subsequently disapproved the Hershey emloyees' organization, the B&C stepped in with a major membership drive. In March 1938, it won an NLRB election by 1,125 to 733 for the CIO, becoming sole bargaining agent for the company's estimated 2,400 to 3,000 employees.

In the course of the 1930s, a broad group of workers and employers gradually became accustomed to dealing with each other on a contractual basis. Many of the strikes of that decade, Dan Conway believed, were simply the result of inexperience; "it was new to everybody, both to the workers and to the management, and there was just constant resistance." As early as the 1936 convention, however, the B&C was hailing "the growing contractual relationship between local union, and employers."

While contract negotiation was still based upon the principle of local autonomy, certain general patterns were emerging. Handicraft shops were maintaining their weekly scales, but mechanized factories were gradually shifting to hourly pay rates. Most local agreements provided for overtime pay at the rate of time and a half over 40 hours in factories, over 48 in the retail shops. Other benefits were still in their infancy, as indicated by the tentative observation of the General Executive Board that a vacation system "undoubtedly deserves serious consideration."

A study of contracts in the baking industry by the U.S. Bureau of Labor Statistics just four years later suggests how far contractual negotiations had matured by that time. Most factories now had classification systems to describe the duties and remuneration for various types of workers, though the BLS found that the descriptive terminology for various jobs varied so much that it was almost impossible to draw comparisons in the wages of workers from firm to firm. Some 60 percent of the agreements provided that all hiring would be done through the union office, and 75 percent contained union label provisions. The eight-hour day had become standard throughout the industry, in small and large enterprises alike. More than half the agreements provided for vacations with pay after a year's continuous employment—usually amounting to one week—and many provided for holidays with pay, six being most common.

Seniority preference in promotions, lay-offs and rehiring had made its way into one-third of the contracts. Many also had embraced work rules prohibiting an employer from requiring bakers to load or unload trucks or perform other tasks not directly related to baking. Much less frequent at this stage were other work rules applying to the number of batches of dough a crew should complete in a shift, the minimum number of workers employed on particular machines or ovens and the amount of relief machine workers could arrange through exchange of jobs with other workers during the day.

One-fifth of the contracts also provided for the appointment of shop stewards from among the regular employees. The novelty of this feature is apparent in a communication from Local 2 of Chicago shortly after it adopted a shop steward system in its 1938 contracts. The local introduced it first into all wholesale plants, but expected to gradually extend it to every shop employing more than two workers. It warned that "fictitious and confusing rumors will be circulated" about the new system. The purpose of the shop steward, it explained, was to enhance the local's control over the shops in order to more rigidly enforce the contract and the union's rules and regulations:

> ...there is every reason to believe that if he be given a reasonable chance, that he will, in time, create in his respective shop among the members an atmosphere of unrestrained freedom and a feeling of unreserved legal right to claim openly in return for their services those things to which they are entitled to under the working agreement which became a legal document when the employer signed same and when the organization affixed its seal to it.

The decade of the Great Depression and the New Deal that had expanded the membership of the B&C and altered the nature of collective bargaining in its jurisdiction also streamlined the International's administration and involved the central office more actively than ever in the field work of the organization. At the highest level, the St. Paul convention in 1941 shed the long aversion to a presidential system of leadership by providing for three national officers—a president and secretary-treasurer, a first vice-president and financial secretary and a second vice-president and corresponding secretary. Andy Myrup for the first time enjoyed clear formal recognition as the leader of the Union, with Winter and Schmidt respectively continuing to fill the remaining two positions. Under this administration in 1941, 20 full-time International field representatives, seven of whom were members of the General Executive Board, now serviced the locals and saw to organizing.

Two months after the St. Paul convention, the United States entered World War II. At the shop floor level, thousands of new workers, primarily women, entered the workforce to replace men who took B&C retiring cards and joined the armed forces or went to work in war industries. By 1943, the B&C counted 21,000 retiring cards and all its locals were reporting large labor turnovers and shortages of help. Employers, claiming that the new employees were inferior workers, sought to place them on lower wage scales, but the B&C locals fought effectively to obtain the same pay for women as for men.

Many business agents and local officers had their hands full trying to keep up with the new workers, becoming, the B&C noted, "application hunters and dues collecting agents," as their rolls shrank to the point that the union's position as representative of the majority of the workers was in jeopardy. By 1943, the International recognized that the problem of "bringing about union and dues paying consciousness to the thousands of strange workers that became employed" had reached alarming proportions. To meet this challenge, the General Executive Board mobilized its field representatives as never before. "We honey-combed every unorganized plant in the United States and Canada," the Board later reported to the 1946 Chicago convention, "not alone in the bread and cake, but in every industry coming under our jurisdiction." The executive officers were constantly in the field themselves, attending conferences and conventions of joint boards, district, state and interstate bodies.

In the heat of this activity, the International suffered the loss of Andy Myrup. The attrition of the old leadership had, of course, been continuing, most notably with the death of Jacob Goldstone after several years of illness in 1940, and Jack Zamford of a stroke in 1941. But when Myrup passed away in his sleep in Boston in the early hours of October 1, 1943, it marked a watershed in the B&C's history. For decades, his large frame, sense of humor and geniality had been a part of the image of solidity, confidence and continuity that he imparted to the organization. The younger leaders had taken this much for granted, with only the stories of the old timers to remind them that stability and unity had not always been the rule in the B&C's national office. Over the next few decades, they would have to learn for themselves how rare these commodities were.

When the General Executive Board met in December 1943 to fill the vacancy left by the death of Myrup, Herman Winter naturally moved into the presidency and Schmidt became first vice-president. Jim Cross might rightfully have expected the appointment as second vice-president, situated as he was in Chicago and in close

William Schnitzler, Herman Winter, and Joe Schmidt.

personal touch with the Board, enjoying a reputation as an inspiring orator and a tough leader. Somewhere in the process, however, he decided to withdraw his name as Bill Schnitzler emerged as the candidate with the inside track.

Schnitzler was no doubt a favorite of Joe Schmidt, a man he regarded as a "father." Schmidt had been the East Coast International representative for many of the years that Schnitzler had been proving his mettle in Newark. He had watched Schnitzler master a precarious labor environment, doing business at the height of Boss Hague's power and under a standing New Jersey injunction against strikes. Schnitzler had learned how to deal directly with employers outside the legal and political constraints—"we were strong-armed guys"—he acknowledged, fighting toe to toe at times against the "hired bums" the employers used for protection. He had also become an astute politician himself, learning to parlay the votes of the bakers' constituency he cultivated in the local saloons and meeting halls into leverage with police headquarters during strikes. Schnitzler had helped make Newark a stronghold for the B&C on the East Coast. This background, combined with his naturally affable outward manner and shrewd and retentive mind helped place him a half step ahead of Cross in the line of succession.

For the time, the challenges of the war were large enough to absorb the talents and ambitions of both these younger leaders. Both spent much of their time helping local unions to negotiate effectively in an environment dominated by the War Labor Board's Little Steel formula, which pegged wage advances to the cost of living. They counseled locals which had already achieved all the WLB was likely to approve in the way of general raises, to make a special case for further raises to bring them up to the level of any neighboring local that enjoyed a higher scale. In addition, they advised them that the WLB would probably accept increases in the form of extra compensation for work during night hours, raising lower-pay classifications to the level of higher classifications to overcome inequities, longer vacations, more paid holidays, liberalization of sick leave practices, shortening of the work week, employer-paid insurance and uniforms, dressing time and the like. These were the difficult issues on the wartime negotiations agenda, Schnitzler told the Midwest bakers' conference in Des Moines in February 1945. While the employers knew that they could always force wages down again after the war, they were afraid that these other concessions "will never be taken away and they know it is just the starting point."

While outwardly Schnitzler and Cross worked at common purposes during these years, it is difficult in retrospect not to wonder to what extent Cross may have carried with him a frustration of thwarted ambition. Of all the younger leaders, his career had advanced the most dramatically and his failure to become an International officer in 1943 must have represented an unaccustomed setback in his mind. On the other hand, it should have been obvious that time in its unrelenting way promised an open field for young men of talent. In 1944, for instance, Executive Board Member Pete Beisel passed away at the age of 69.

If the decision of 1943 did not embitter Cross, the decision of 1946 might have. At the Chicago convention that year, Joe Schmidt retired at the age of 76; he died the following year. At this point Schnitzler engineered a consolidation of the B&C's top positions. Winter now held the post of president; Schnitzler was secretary-treasurer. The third post, that no doubt would have gone to Cross, was abolished. It is possible that Schnitzler meant this move, as he later explained, as a means of streamlining the B&C in the manner of most other unions. Streamlining, after all, was to become a hallmark of Schnitzler's leadership in other ways. But it is equally possible that Schnitzler, as crafty as he was shrewd, may already have perceived a more than normal ambition in Cross and seized the opportunity to hold him at bay.

Edward Stack left his job at Kelley Baking Company in Syracuse, New York, as one of many bakers who practiced their trade for the armed forces during World War II.

7

A Modern but Troubled Union

"If there is any formula for successful labor leadership, the basic ingredient is humility. A leader in organized labor is created by his union's members. If he should lose contact with their thinking and their feelings, a vital circuit is broken and he has lost his only source of strength." (From an editorial by Jim Cross, Bakers' *Journal, February 1953)*

The war was over and John Geiger, International vice-president for the B&C's third district, was reminiscing about the old days. Speaking at the fall 1947 meeting of the B&C's Pennsylvania State Board, he looked back to the days when the "German element" dominated the organization. The changes he had seen in the last decade and a half were all for the better, and the future looked bright in the hands of the new leaders. "They are younger and they've got more sense than we had at the time," he confessed. "They have more education than the German element had at that time."

Geiger's graciousness aside, however, there was a wellspring of experience and a tradition of responsibility in that old leadership that set a standard the postwar generation could embrace with pride. Many years later, Wes Reedy would rethink his initial impatience with the oldtimers. "The International officers had an organization that they were devoted to, it was their baby," he realized. "They knew of the trials and tribulations of the past, they were quite concerned about the present, and not knowing the multitude of new young local union officers, they were very much concerned about the future."

Most likely because Herman Winter seemed to symbolize the B&C's ties with this past, he became the honored patriarch of the Union's postwar years. Born in the mid-1880s, a baker's helper at

Herman Winter

the age of 12 and a member of Local 218 in Kansas City from 1902, he had steadily served the organization for four and a half decades. He had been on the General Executive Board when the last great war was fought, serving from 1911 to 1921, and had returned to the inner circle of leadership on Charles Hohmann's death in 1936. When the bakers of New York threw a testimonial dinner in his honor on George Washington's birthday in 1947, they seemed to be reaching out to reaffirm the organization's ties to its earlier generations. The honors extended to him that day, they proclaimed, "will be of lasting impression and spiritual encouragement. . . ."

Winter had presided over the B&C as the war nudged the locals further than ever from the earlier tradition of local autonomy. As Wes Reedy pointed out, contract negotiations until that time had involved local unions drafting their demands and presenting them directly to the employers in their jurisdiction. In the larger cities, the local's negotiating committee would generally meet with a group of employers who were members of the local bakers' association to negotiate an agreement covering all bakeries in the city. In reality, however, a large national chain bakery like Continental was in a position to exert a commanding influence over the other bakeries. In Philadelphia, Reedy explained, "the settlement in most every instance was actually dictated by Continental." Jim Cross confirmed the same reality, telling the Pennsylvania State Board in 1949 that Continental's power to direct wage negotiations came from its ability "to walk into your localities and say to those independent baker[s], 'Either you give what we tell you to give or we are going out and put you out of business.'"

As early as the St. Paul convention in 1941, therefore, the B&C recommended that locals consider chain-wide or company-wide bargaining. By 1943, Herman Winter thought the preconditions for this development were virtually in place. He calculated that the International was on the verge of completely unionizing the giants of the wholesale trade. Seventy of Continental's 83 plants were under contract, 44 of General's 45, 18 of Schults' 19, and 45 of Purity's 47. He believed that national agreements were now feasible, possibly embodying a union-shop clause and grievance system, with wages and hours determined locally or by districts or zones. Negotiating such agreements, he argued, would enable strong locals to provide

126

an umbrella of protection for weaker locals and would result in a better contract than any local might negotiate separately.

Gradually, broader-based negotiations began to materialize. In the cracker and biscuit industry, five B&C locals and one AFL Federal Labor Union negotiated jointly with Nabisco as early as 1941. In October 1944, representatives from Nabisco locals in 11 cities jointly negotiated a contract covering nearly 10,000 workers. Meanwhile, bread locals in the ninth and tenth district councils on the West Coast were engaging in limited joint negotiations by war's end.

In a parallel development, two statewide negotiation efforts began in the Midwest. In September 1945, Jim Cross urged delegates to the Illinois State Bakers' Council to consider instituting statewide contract negotiations, and the *Bakers' Journal* reported that on May 23, 1946, after several months of "intensive, nerve wracking negotiations," employers signed a statewide contract affecting 14 locals with a membership of 1,500. When the Pennsylvania State Board met in August, Bill Schnitzler proclaimed that 21 Illinois locals were now covered by one contract that affected all of the state's wholesale bakeries and that all the retail bakeries in the state of Illinois were on strike for a similar purpose. He also announced that the Wisconsin State Board had begun planning statewide negotiations.

In the postwar period, the composition of the B&C continued to change, as it had throughout its history. It absorbed large numbers of blacks and hispanics who entered the industries it represented. It also penetrated the South. This was the preserve of Curtis Sims, former president of the Chattanooga Central Labor Union and leader of that town's Local 25. A maverick with a freewheeling but tenacious style, Sims was at his best when taking individual locals under his wing and guiding them through organizing campaigns and negotiations. He ignored headquarters with impunity when it came to obtaining permission to strike or keeping expenditures within guidelines that he regarded as "tight fisted," and had little interest in establishing within his domain the joint negotiations that were becoming popular elsewhere. Nevertheless, he maintained his undisputed hold on his territory by getting results. Herman Winter knew what conditions had been like before the B&C launched its serious assault on the South in 1938. He recalled in 1945, that in one shop he had visited before unionization took hold, only one of 80 workers was able to write his name. "These people were earning such miserably low wages that even the most elementary education was a great luxury," he commented.

To say that Sims single-handedly organized the South would be an overstatement. Certainly he benefited immensely from the unionization of A&P, facilitated by an understanding the B&C reached with the giant grocery chain in Scranton. In exchange for the Union's cooperation in opposing the Patman bill before Congress—designed to combat chain-store competitive practices—the B&C gained free access to the workers in A&P bakery plants throughout the country. Successful organization of A&P plants in the South often provided a core union membership that could sustain further organizing activities.

Much of the South, however, still had to be organized by scratching away in one hostile town after another, and for that, as the *American Federationist* recognized, Sims was "chiefly responsible." By 1947, the B&C had a substantial presence in the South. Sims, with three organizers under his direction, had brought in tens of thousands in a section where an average wholesaler had no more than 75 workers. Where some establishments had paid as little as 15 cents an hour prior to unionization, wage rates in organized plants now ranged from 65 cents to $1.40 an hour.

William Schnitzler

Under his direction Sims had A.B. Searcy, whom the *American Federationst* described as "an energetic, sincere young Negro unionist who came out of the trade in Savannah, Georgia." With a "strict no-discrimination policy" the B&C's rank and file in the South was 40 percent black. "Negro and white wage rates are the same," Sims claimed. "We have Negro head bakers and Negro foremen and foreladies. They supervise white and Negro workers. We have Negro owners employing white workers and we bargain with the Negro employers for the white workers...." Only where black workers insisted on separate locals and had sufficient members to justify it did Sims install separate locals based on race. In 1947, there were only three of these, one each in Savannah, Charleston and Wilmington. All other Southern locals were racially mixed.

While Herman Winter's leadership of the B&C took on a symbolic character in the late 1940's, providing an emotional link to the older generation of leaders, Winter in fact gradually ceded most duties to Bill Schnitzler, 20 years his junior. Perhaps some of the drive went out of the older leader as early as 1940, after the death of his wife of 33 years. He also suffered from a serious skin disease that required debilitating treatments. In 1948, he relocated to Kansas City and Schnitzler became president in everything but name. The General Executive Board at the same time named Jim Cross as assistant general secretary-treasurer and Curt Sims as director of organization to work with Schnitzler. Two years later Winter retired and Schnitzler began his brief two-year tenure as B&C president, Cross taking the number two position.

The years between 1948 and 1952 were foundation years for some of the most important features of the B&C. Under the new leadership team, the B&C expanded its efforts to establish joint negotiations with chain bakeries. To Jim Cross's mind, negotiation with a single multi-city firm appeared easier to accomplish than joint negotiations with all employers in a given state or region. Speaking to the Pennsylvania State Board on his experience with the Illinois state negotiations he claimed that rank and file members simply were not willing to risk their contract and job "to take care of the Podunk Cake Shop down in Louisville, Kentucky." On the other hand, the workers at Hostess Cake Company at one location seemed quite willing "to go to bat and combine their forces to help every other Hostess Cake Shop in the United States."

In December 1949, the General Executive Board convened a conference of Continental locals and established the Continental Division with Wes Reedy as chairman and Louis Genuth of New York City Local 50 as secretary. "The early conferences were—to put it

The General Executive Board in 1950. Left to Right First Row: Seb Ollinger, James Cross, William Schnitzler, William McGuern, William Schumacher; Second Row: George Stuart, Robert Hart, Harvey Friedman, Aurelio Irizarry, James Landriscina, Sven Jensen; Third Row: Wesley Reedy, Peter Olson, Daniel Conway, John Simmons, Amos Miller, Sam Wehofer, Max Kralstein.

mildly, quite hectic," Reedy related, "mainly because of the reluctance of the local unions to relinquish autonomy and thus be governed by a majority vote of Continental members throughout the country. . . ." Over the next two years, the B&C established other divisions covering Ward, General, Purity-Grennan, Purity of Illinois and Hathaway.

On June 17, 1952, the National Labor Relations Board threw up a roadblock to divisional bargaining. The Taft-Hartley Act of 1947 had signaled a shift in the legal climate of the country insofar as it affected collective bargaining. Continental's attorneys were able to convince the B&C that union efforts to force divisional bargaining through strikes could now be effectively resisted through court injunctions and damage suits against locals all over the country; these would tie the issue up in litigation for years at the cost to the Union of millions of dollars In a compromise arranged through Cyrus Ching, Director of the Federal Conciliation Service, the firm and the Union agreed to consolidate the issue into one case to go before the NLRB.

As late as November 1951, Herbert Thatcher, the attorney representing the B&C, felt confident that the Union would win the case. "I have been in a lot of Labor Board cases," he assured the Union, ". . . and I can in all honesty say this: I have never had such a profound conviction as to the absolute merits of a cause. . . ." He could not see how the Board could rule against the B&C. The Board, nevertheless, did rule against the Union, deciding that the chain-wide division was not an appropriate unit, acceding to the argument that such a unit defied the long tradition of local association bargaining established in the industry.

Behind the decision, as Bill Schnitzler pointed out, was an unfortunate series of developments. Of the five-man NLRB, the individual most favorable to the B&C's position could not participate in the case because his wife had a relative working in Continental's Kansas City plant. The disqualification of one member of the Board left four; since the Board had a standing rule of only sitting with an odd number of members in order to avoid a tie vote, a second member, also sympathetic with the B&C position, dropped out of the case. The remaining members voted two to one in favor of Continental.

The decision of the Board, however, did not mean that collective bargaining returned to its older localized pattern. For one thing, Continental understood that it had won a slender victory in a truncated board, not a definitive determination of the issue. For another, the divisional experience had served an important educating purpose, convincing local union officers of what Reedy had been calling the "bankruptcy of local union bargaining...." Bill Schnitzler made clear the B&C's belief that "there is no company in the baking industry I know of, that can stop our membership from winning company-wide contracts if our membership decides that is what they want." Divisional meetings continued and proved particularly useful in establishing common rallying points for negotiations. The B&C, though, eventually began to rely more upon regional bargaining in which all locals in defined multi-state areas could coordinate their negotiations with large wholesalers as well as local bakers' associations.

If Bill Schnitzler's tenure at the helm of the B&C marked the foundation years for centralized bargaining, it also saw the advent of a new style of leadership. Schnitzler was a strong and innovative leader, understanding the power of his position and willing to use it in Executive Board meetings and in the committees of the conventions to advocate new directions. He personally identified himself with the goal of achieving employee health and welfare and pension programs and led the 1951 convention in initiating the studies that inaugurated the B&C's national plans a few years later.

At the same time, in Schnitzler the International had a leader who was a "road man," an experienced and imaginative organizer and negotiator who, as president, continued to personally visit local and state conventions, go drinking with the boys, and know men in every local by name. His own example instilled confidence in the organizers on the B&C staff as did his insistence on putting their service on a more professional basis. He saw to it that those who went on the road for the International no longer had to sleep in flop houses; he increased their expense allowances, furnished decent automobiles to get them around and established a health and welfare program and a pension system for officers and staff.

The news in late 1952 that the AFL's new president, George Meany, had personally tapped Bill Schnitzler to be the AFL's secretary-treasurer, was stunning, pride of the moment mixed with understanding of a void the Bakers would now have to fill. It was "Big Bill's" day. Time to play Baker Bill to the rush of press interest. Was he pleased with his appointment as secretary-treasurer? He'd rather stay where he was. "I'm a baker, and I want to stay with it." The trouble was, they had kept calling him back, telling him he had nothing to say about it. "They didn't pay any attention to me.... I'm overwhelmed and I'm unhappy about the whole thing." In fact the big event in his life that day, he insisted, was not his appointment but the fact that after nine years, he had finally obtained a recipe for a banana pecan nut cake served at a Hot Springs, Arkansas, restaurant; "got it from the daughter of the chef," he confided.

Schnitzler later looked back on his departure from the the B&C. After turning the reins over to Jim Cross in December 1952, Schnitzler remembered sitting on his bed for an hour or so, unable to go to sleep. "I put the wrong guy in," he told his wife. Yet who else could he have suggested? Whatever reservations Schnitzler may have had at the time, few others would have shared them. Cross had a personal following in the organization that was possibly second only to Schnitzler's. Perhaps it was no longer second at all, for as the leader of the move to centralized bargaining, Schnitzler had aroused some enmity from those who embraced the B&C's long tradition of local autonomy. Cross, at the same time, had developed close relations with many Board members as well as extensive contacts with the rank and file, having traveled the country for the B&C. A spellbinding speaker with the sharpest of minds, he seemed destined not only for the B&C presidency but for higher office in the labor movement some day.

There was a story Jim Cross told the Pennsylvania State Board back in October 1949 that would not have seemed fraught with

William Schnitzler and George Meany, the new leaders of the AFL,
featured on the January 1953 cover of the Bakers' and Confectioners'
Journal.

deeper meaning at the time. The DC-3 ride in, Cross would have
his listeners believe, had been especially eventful. "There was only
the stewardess and I on that plane, and we really did some hopping
around. (Laughter) The big trouble with that was that we had to
keep our seat belts on the whole trip because it was a little rocky.
(Laughter) Further explanations will be given in private (Laughter)."
While the story was just a tickler Cross used to warm up his au-

dience, it hinted at the seamier private side of Cross that the bakers only gradually came to know.

For now, however, there seemed little reason to question Cross' profession in his first editorial in 1953 that the B&C was an "heirloom" he would handle with "cautious respect." He reassured his readers that "the responsibility and integrity of this International never have fallen under the shadow of questioning." At the same time he made clear the duty of "patriotic" members to tolerate neither dishonesty nor disloyalty to the B&C. There was no reason as yet to ask what loyalty required when national leadership did fall under the shadow of questioning.

For his first three or four years, Cross built on Schnitzler's legacy to install some of the most important and lasting features of the modern B&C. Joint negotiations continued to prove their viability. In the spring of 1952, the Purity of Illinois Division became the first to achieve recognition and certification as a collective bargaining unit and the first to negotiate a comprehensive health and welfare plan. George Stuart, who had worked with Herman Winter in Kansas City and succeeded Jim Cross as sixth district vice-president in 1949, chaired this division as well as the Purity-Grennan division. A stocky, tough looking individual who always wore a smile but also packed a revolver, he would soon emerge as Cross' trusted road man and ally.

More important than the single breakthrough at Purity of Illinois was the process of regular coordination of collective bargaining that took hold by the middle of the decade. Delegates representing the B&C's six company divisions met in St. Louis in December 1952 and established five rallying points: a five-day week with three weeks' vacation after five years of employment, improved night work compensation, increased wages and employer paid health and welfare plans. The following year they expanded their goals to include a 35-hour week, employer-paid pension plans and a clause shielding members from the effects of mechanization. Cross presented a model mechanization clause a few months later. It provided that workers would not lose their employment or job classification or suffer reduced pay because of mechanization, that increased productive capacity would be grounds for renegotiation of wage rates and that differences concerning new wage rates would be subject to arbitration. In 1954, the General Executive Board took another step in restructuring collective bargaining by dividing the Union into five regional conferences for the purpose of developing more uniform contract demands and more effective cooperation.

By 1954, when B&C negotiators spoke of welfare and pensions

134

they had very specific plans in mind. On May 14, 1953, the B&C formally ratified a national welfare fund providing life, health and hospital insurance. Based on the "pool principle," it called for employers to contribute to a national fund administered by seven trustees, three from the Union, three from management and one neutral. Members were eligible for benefits according to a schedule based upon their employers' contributions. The plan freed locals to concentrate on the negotiation of employer contributions without getting involved in the administration of the program. Furthermore its mass purchasing principle, combined with lower administrative costs for the Union and the insurance company, provided substantial savings in members' health costs. The plan was so attractive that the B&C was able to phase out its older sick and death benefit at the 25th convention in San Francisco in 1956.

In March 1955, the General Executive Board adopted a national pension fund based on a similar model. In addition to economies of centralization and scale, which lowered administrative costs and allowed for more diversified investments, the fund provided workers with vested security and continuity in contributions should they change jobs and move to another plant covered by the fund. Further savings came from administering the pension fund from the same offices that conducted welfare fund operations.

At the time that Jim Cross took over the presidency of the B&C, Curtis Sims moved up to become secretary-treasurer and Dan Conway—West Coast vice-president since 1948—came to Chicago as director of organization. Conway set about instituting a new organization program that involved dividing the United States into four organizing regions and Canada into two, each to be handled by a well-coordinated team of organizers. "No longer will we be content to assign one man to a campaign or a city and let him work and strive to complete that assignment," Conway explained. As part of the emphasis on coordination and planning, Conway called the entire organizing staff of the International together in October 1953 for a two day meeting at the Webster Hotel in Chicago "to map plans for future activities...."

The new organizing approach appeared especially auspicious for the attention it focused on Canada. In 1951, less than 4,000 of the B&C's approximately 170,000 members were in Canada. Some of the Canadian locals had long, but for the most part erratic, histories. Toronto bakers had formed a strong Knights of Labor assembly in the late 19th century and had been part of the B&C in the early years of the 20th century, but by 1913 they, as well as bakers in Winnipeg and several other cities, had withdrawn from the International to explore establishing a national organization in connection with the Canadian Federation of Labour. The B&C had only Jewish Local 181 in Toronto, Local 115 in Montreal and Local 179 in Vancouver by this date. Other Toronto bakers joined the B&C in 1914 as Local 268, but the bakers' movement remained divided and weak into the post World War I period. Vancouver bakers disbanded their local after an unsuccessful strike in 1920 and did not reorganize as Local 468 until 1925. It wasn't until the following decade that it negotiated its first contract. Montreal Local 115 maintained its organization but, as financial secretary A. Suffrin reflected in 1951, since joining the B&C "we have had our ups and downs, mostly the latter...."

During the 1930s, Suffrin served on the General Executive Board from the eleventh district and urged greater attention to Canadian organization. Militantly active organizations such as Hamilton Local 72 and Toronto Local 131 achieved substantial success. The initiative, however, still rested with the locals and their city trades and labor councils rather than with the International. It was only in the later years of World War II that the B&C began to give more serious, sustained and methodical attention to Canadian organizing, appointing several organizers to cover the provinces. Conway's program in the early 1950s built upon this initiative.

Amid this swirl of activity and accomplishment, it was only insiders at first who became concerned with the style of leadership of Jim Cross. Behind the air of confidence and authority that Cross projected, appears to have been an unusually insecure individual. Wes Reedy, who served as assistant to the president under Schnitzler and Cross, recalled an incident following a farewell luncheon for Schnitzler that epitomized Cross' relations with his associates. "Well fellows it's going to be a new ballgame," Reedy recalled Cross announcing. As Reedy reconstructed it, Cross then "went on to say that he expects 100 percent dedication and loyalty from everyone working on his staff. All the staff was asked to pledge their loyalty. . . ."

Cross seemed unable to shake the shadow of his predecessor. John DeConcini, whom Schnitzler brought forward as an International vice-president in 1952, depicted Cross as evincing a "terrible dislike" for Schniztler and seizing every opportunity at meetings of the General Executive Board to blame things on him. Organizer Marty Bacon believed that the merger of the AFL and the CIO in 1955 aggravated these feelings. According to Bacon, the merger created the specter in Cross' mind that the CIO's Walter Reuther would replace Schnitzler as the number two man in the merged organization and that Schnitzler would seek to return to the Bakers' presidency.

Cross' style in office in someways mimicked Schnitzler's and in someways turned the function of the presidency on its head. Schnitzler and Cross to a great extent both exemplified the Bakers' leaders who had come of age during the Depression and the New Deal. The experience imbued that generation with expectations of dramatic results and established an unrelenting pace as their norm. It was labor leadership on the fast track. Schnitzler proved to be the most flamboyant national leader in any baker's memory, not afraid to spend money in support of the officers and staff upon whose work the organization's rapid progress depended. The crucial difference between him and Cross on this account was one of degree. Schnitzler created a new sense of freedom in the use of the Union's resources; Cross lacked the character to use this freedom with responsibility and self-restraint.

In addition, it soon became clear to insiders that Cross did not intend to be a road man. He increasingly saw his role as dealing directly with employers on the golf course or in New York City and Miami. "Cross would talk about meeting with this employer or with that group of employers," Wes Reedy related, "and comment on what a tremendous job he was doing in organizing, meeting with employers, and attorneys, and so forth." He delegated to Reedy the handling of everyday office matters during his absences.

In July 1955, Reedy left the B&C to become Bill Schnitzler's assistant at the AFL; the same month the B&C moved the office of its president to Washington, D.C., in part because of the need for greater space at headquarters, in part because the Taft-Hartley Act made it more convenient than ever to be on hand at the nation's capital to deal regularly with matters before the National Labor Relations Board, the Department of Labor and other federal agencies. The B&C rented offices at 1145 Nineteenth Street, N.W.

Cross took the opportunity to bring in two of his closest supporters. One was George Stuart, who became director of organization, Dan Conway moving over to the new office of administrative director. The other was Lester Crawford, who had worked with Cross in organizing Nabisco in St. Louis. He now came to the president's office in charge of special assignments, particularly the affiliation of various CIO bakers' unions with the B&C after the merger of the AFL and the CIO. Crawford was to serve as a liaison for closer coordination among the four regional conferences. In October 1955, the B&C closed the Chicago headquarters completely, moving the office of secretary-treasurer to Washington.

It was in late 1955 that rumors began to circulate that Cross had been siphoning off Union funds for his own personal purposes. The source of these rumors was Curtis Sims who, as secretary-treasurer, had to approve vouchers and checks. Having himself resisted what he regarded as tight-fisted handling of the treasury when he was a field worker, Sims may have been too cavalier at first about the expenditures his own signature helped authorize. Nevertheless, what were apparently only echoes of his private grumblings in late 1955 were on the brink of becoming public charges against Cross by 1956. The evening prior to the assembling of the General Executive Board in Washington in July 1956, Sims laid out evidence he had been accumulating to a group of about seven Board members at a dinner at the Normandy Farms restaurant. The group reached the consensus that Sims would bring the charges into the open the following day and that the group would back him up.

Somewhere in the course of the next day, however, Sims changed his mind. As John DeConcini reconstructed the day, the Board spent the morning on routine business and adjourned for lunch. The convening of the afternoon meeting was delayed by three hours, however, as Cross, Sims and Herman Winter—who as president emeritus attended all Board meetings—held private discussions in another room. When they returned, the issue had been buried; Sims, sitting on hard evidence of Cross' malfeasance, said nothing. Later he explained to DeConcini that Winter had persuaded him that presenting the charges would split the Union; Cross had promised to clean up the problem and Winter had assured Sims that he would personally oversee the process of reform. Sims was also convinced, according to Henry Alvino, that most of the members of the Board were "in Cross' hip pocket," either personally loyal to him or beholden to him for some of the many favors he had learned to distribute that sometimes enmeshed people as co-conspirators almost before they fully realized what was happening to them.

In failing to bring the issue to a head at this point, Sims paved the way for a bizarre and ultimately tragic series of events. By late 1956, Cross seems to have been overcome by a siege mentality. Not only were there serious charges circulating against him, but Harvey Friedman had begun canvassing for the B&C presidency on the supposition that the 1956 convention would depose Cross. An indication of Cross' frame of mind was the so-called "midnight raid" at the San Francisco convention. Details concerning this incident emerged from the hearings of the United States Senate Select Committee on Improper Activities in the Labor or Management Field, also known as the Senate rackets committee, chaired by John L.

McClellan in 1957. It appears that Cross, accompanied by strong-armed supporters George Stuart, Frank Gardone and Frank Mykalo, beat up New York opposition leaders Joe Kane, Louis Genuth and Nathan Ehrlich, along with Ehrlich's wife, in their hotel rooms. A San Francisco grand jury later failed to find that a case existed against Cross and his supporters, complaining that the testimony of witnesses and alleged participants on both sides was "rampant with perjury."

Henry Kaiser, an attorney on the scene at San Francisco who later worked for Bakers' leaders opposed to Cross, recalled that the case dissolved when the investigating detective suddenly decided to go on vacation; Kaiser recalled that attorney Herman Cooper "handled" the San Francisco case. Cooper over the next few years served as the legal strategist in Cross' gambit to keep control of the B&C. Cross later swore before the McClellan committee that he was taking a shower in his room at the time of the disturbance. The committee found Cross guilty of perjury for this testimony, but Cross, defended by Attorney Edward Bennett Williams, gained acquittal in federal court in 1959 on the grounds that the committee exceded its authority since its investigation went beyond what was necessary for its purpose of framing labor legislation.

While the melee at the San Francisco convention received widespread newspaper coverage and national attention, in the next few days Cross was able to turn the event to his advantage among the delegates and emerge from the convention in a stronger position than ever. According to Dan Conway, there was a good deal of prejudice against the New York delegates, a feeling that they had always caused trouble at conventions. Henry Alvino confirmed that the people who accused Cross were generally unpopular. Joe Kane, who had led the New York Sunshine biscuit workers from 1941 to 1949 in the CIO and afterwards in affiliation with the B&C, seems particularly to have had a reputation as a rebel—stemming, John DeConcini explained, from his strong opposition to the administration at the 1951 convention. The convention therefore rallied around its besieged president. It gave him the power to appoint 12 of the 17 members of the Board as salaried International representatives and gave the Board the power to set officers' salaries. The Board, now composed of a majority serving as representatives at Cross' pleasure at annual salaries of $11,150 to $15,000, voted to raise the president's salary from $17,500 to $30,000. Cross then approved raises for various Board members.

Cross, who spent an increasing amount of his time at a Palm Springs home he had recently purchased, left Washington at the beginning of 1957 to spend three months in Florida on a "combination of business and vacation." On his return to Washington, however, he faced charges by Sims who had finally decided to come out in the open with the facts he had accumulated. Behind Sims by this point was a group of four vice-presidents who in February joined him in forming the Committee to Preserve Integrity. The committee included Sims, Conway, DeConcini, Archie Goodman—district nine vice-president out of Los Angeles Local 37, and Amos Miller—who had taken over for Curtis Sims in the South. The committee retained Henry Kaiser, who gave his legal services at no cost, and drew up a series of eight charges which it mailed directly to the B&C's locals and gave to the press on March 3. Later in the month, Sims testified in more detail on Cross' dealings before the McClellan committee.

These actions opened the book on Cross' activities. There were personal expenses, including long-distance phone calls to Kate Lower, a West Coast woman whom Los Angeles police identified as a convicted prostitute, and thousands of dollars in inadequately documented vouchers. In 1956, alone, his unsubstantiated vouchers for travel, entertainment, dinners, birthday parties, gratuities and personal expenses came to $39,682. There were two Cadillacs driven by Cross and George Stuart, supposedly gifts from a Detroit Teamsters' local but in fact paid for by money Stuart siphoned from the treasury of Chicago Local 1, over which Stuart was trustee. Evidence suggested that Stuart had sent $13,100.18 to a Detroit Teamsters' local for a joint organizing campaign, and the Teamsters local had in turn delivered the two vehicles, each bearing the price tag of $6,550.09. In addition there were loans totalling $112,700 to Cross from the family of Martin Philipsborn, owner of Zion Industries, Inc., to help Cross pay for his Palm Beach house. Cross had aborted a threatening strike situation at Zion and perpetuated a substandard contract. In light of these dealings, along with Cross' denial of his involvement in the San Francisco midnight raid, Sims called for a General Executive Board trial of the B&C president.

On March 6, however, Cross countered by bringing charges against Sims. Cross claimed that Sims' public charges had damaged the B&C by discrediting its good name and undermining its dignity "in a public climate particularly hostile to labor leaders charged with dishonesty." Sims' charges were mere allegations, Cross pointed out, designed to undermine himself and Stuart for Sims' own personal purposes. Furthermore, Sims had caused "unwarranted and unnecessary expense" by requiring the B&C to convene a special Board meeting despite the fact that the Board was scheduled to hold a regular meeting on March 20.

The special session of the Board met March 6th through 8th, chaired by Conway, with DeConcini as hearing secretary. It acquitted Cross of all charges, two by unanimous agreement, the remaining six with a small minority of five board members voting to convict. On March 27, the Board reconvened at the Monte Carlo Hotel in Miami Beach to consider the charges against Sims. Cross reached deep within himself for the forensic display he launched at the Monte Carlo. He excoriated Sims for departing from the long tradition of "awareness that unions and their leaders could not expect a hostile press or an uninformed public to judge the merits of conduct by union officials." Sims had taken the issue outside the "family of organization" and the "ground rules plainly stated by the Constitution" and opened the B&C to "harmful and unwarranted public scandal and disrepute" that hampered the effectiveness of the organization.

In Cross' view, Sims was a secretive and power-hungry individual. Depicting Sims as a self-appointed secret service who engaged in "two years of secret investigations, taking photostats, going from this section of the country to the other in order to obtain secret information against an officer," Cross pointed out that Sims "approved the vouchers that he now complains of. . ..He signed the checks. . .." Noting that Sims claimed to have discovered the transgressions as early as March 1956, he wondered why Sims had remained silent at Board meetings in March, July and October of 1956 and at the San Francisco convention. "I think it is clear and obvious that his real purpose was not innocent or commendable, but designed to discredit and destroy the International President. . .so he could achieve his personal ambition of becoming the president of this International Union; otherwise there's no real explanation for what he has done. . . ."

Finally Cross accused Sims of trying to destroy his family "in attempting to expose and intimate that I was keeping relationship with a person of ill repute. . . ." In this, Sims failed to reckon with the fact that "Myself and my wife and child are trade unionists. . . . They have been and I have been since the day we were born into a coal mining union family. . . . " Sims' charges could not shake his family's loyalty, he exulted, but were still reprehensible. "No man attempts to destroy a man's family regardless of what happens. Thankfully, I have a wife and child that were schooled in trade unionism, and know how to stand up under these circumstances. Let Sims sleep with himself for the rest of his life."

In a secret ballot, a majority of the Executive Board proceeded to find Sims guilty of the charges and to suspend him for three months, pending a decision on a penalty; it dismissed him in September. Following the Board meeting, Herman Winter sent a personal letter to B&C locals testifying to the fairness of the proceedings that upheld Cross and Stuart and found Sims guilty. "This is the democratic, trade-union way of settling internal disputes," he assured the locals. Sims could only observe that "most of my judges are employed by my accuser, and all of them are subject to economic gain or loss by his favor or displeasure."

The Jimmy Cross story broke in the midst of a movement at the national level to deal with widely publicized corruption in some labor unions. While the McClellan hearings wound their way toward inevitable federal regulation, embodied in the Landrum-Griffin Act of 1959, the AFL-CIO instituted a self-policing mechanism through its Ethical Practices Committee. By the time of Sims' suspension, members of the B&C Committee to Preserve Integrity believed that Cross would never be able to satisfy the AFL-CIO's housecleaning requirements, that Cross would never willingly step down, and that the most likely scenario would involve Cross trying to lead a B&C independently of the AFL-CIO or in affiliation with the Teamsters Union. Cross had a long friendship with Teamsters' President Jimmy Hoffa, stemming back to the days when each worked for his respective union in Detroit, and it was clear that the Teamsters' problems with corruption would force it out of the AFL-CIO by year's end.

In the months after Sims' suspension, therefore, the integrity committee set out to build support among the locals for an alternate bakers' movement that would remain with the AFL-CIO after Cross took the B&C out of it. While Cross did not seek immediately to remove any of the committee's members other than Sims from the B&C payroll, Dan Conway took a leave of absence without pay rather than continue in his job at headquarters. Conway, as the leading B&C officer on the integrity committee, as well as an individual with some college education behind him, emerged as the leader of the group. Not a gregarious person, he presented a somewhat remote but mild-mannered and dignified image which, with his dedication and scrupulous honesty, was well suited for the work of running a national office. The committee's support came from locals in small donations. With this, the committee paid its expenses, including support for Sims and Conway, who were no longer on the B&C payroll. The road work of the committee was primarily DeConcini's domain, secondarily Sims'. DeConcini later recalled the heart of his message to locals in these months: "Your president is going to go to jail."

Throughout 1957, Cross tried to create a public image of a Union mending its ways. He retained James Rowe, a close friend of Lyndon Johnson, to represent him as counsel before the AFL-CIO Ethical Practices Committee and in the McClellan hearings of the Senate. In March, the B&C General Executive Board adopted the AFL-CIO Code of Ethics "in all respects" and required "vigorous and vigilant enforcement" from its officers. It directed its general counsel, Herman Cooper, to distribute a questionnaire that would ferret out any current practices that constituted a breach of ethics. Cross paid back some of the funds he had drawn for questionable purposes and returned the Cadillac that had drawn such unfavorable notice. He conducted a tour of B&C locals to explain the "conspiracy against him." In May, Cross hired Professor David Brown of George Washington University and three other academic management consultants to study the B&C's internal affairs and recommend improvements. The professors gave the B&C good grades, though Murray Kempton of the *New York Post*, noting that Brown had never interviewed such key critics as Sims, called the report "the garbage to be expected of management surveys thus conducted in the abstract. . . ."

On October 20, Harvey Friedman, throwing his support behind Cross, conducted a special conference at the Hotel Carter in Cleveland. The meeting, attended by about 300 delegates from 96 locals, was closed to the press. Friedman reported that the delegates gave a rising vote of confidence to Cross and added that "regardless of any errors he might have made in judgment or regardless of any mistakes he has made, his dynamic leadership and his keen judgment are most essential to the progress and well being of our international union." In the streets, 150 B&C members from 40 to 45 locals picketed with signs reading "Cross must Go." DeConcini, who led the pickets, was able to convince a number of the delegates not to go through the picket lines and they eventually affiliated with the Conway group.

In the meantime, the AFL-CIO had been moving inexorably to a full confrontation with Cross. In September, the Ethical Practices Committee reported to the Federation's Executive Council that Cross had engaged in unethical practices in violation of the AFL-CIO constitution through his financial relationship to an officer of a company with which he bargained, receipt of substantial gifts from a local under trusteeship, the questionable manner of accounting for his expenses, and failure to take action to have George Stuart expelled for diversion of B&C funds to private use. The Executive Council endorsed the report and gave the B&C one month "to eliminate corrupt influences from the Union and to remove and bar from any position or office either appointive or elective, in the International Union, or in any of its subordinate bodies, those who are responsible for these abuses...."

On October 4, the B&C adopted reforms designed to blunt, if not to completely meet, the AFL-CIO's demands. It prohibited locals under trusteeship from spending money on testimonial dinners or gifts and provided for periodic review of such locals by impartial observers. It also elected a committee of three vice-presidents to audit the accounts of local unions that had been under George Stuart's control; the committee reported that Stuart had improperly used funds of two locals under his trusteeship. Finally, the B&C gave the power to remove Executive Board members to the Board itself. These reforms formed the core of the Union's response to the AFL-CIO Executive Council on October 18.

For the rest, the B&C denied that the Ethical Practices Committee report had demonstrated "irredeemable guilt" of the sort that would destroy the ability of any of its officers to continue serving the Union. "This is an honest union," it contended, "and its officials have never been charged with involvement with racketeers or extortionists, mulcting health and welfare funds, chartering paper locals, improper imposition of trusteeship or use of union funds for personal investment." Cross' shortcomings, it suggested, were errors of judgment that he had already rectified and that would be avoided in the future through changes in procedures for handling expense accounts. In addition, the AFL-CIO should consider the manner in which Sims had gathered and presented his charges at a "politically convenient time" and with a haste that "deprived the board of an opportunity for making an independent investigation to ascertain the accuracy of his allegations."

On October 23, the AFL-CIO Executive Council rejected the B&C's position. It demanded that the B&C reinstate Sims and call a special convention within 90 days to hold an election of officers in which those individuals whom the Ethical Practices Committee identified as responsible for abuses would be ineligible to run. The B&C's rejection of these terms resulted in its suspension from the AFL-CIO on November 14, paving the way for a final confrontation at the Federation's Atlantic City convention in December.

While Cross moved toward an impasse with the AFL-CIO, he conspicuously courted the Teamsters during the fall of 1957. Cross invited Jimmy Hoffa to the meeting of the B&C General Executive Board in Cincinnati in September, and the Teamsters' leader assured the B&C that the two unions would go down the path together. On October 31, Cross sent a circular to B&C locals telling them that the B&C's decision on how to respond to the AFL-CIO's directives would be "dictated solely by you and your interests" and would not disturb the members' working conditions or union benefits "so long as we remain united." Anticipating the results of his policies, he contended that "other international unions have grown and flourished without affiliation with the AFL-CIO," referring to the disaffiliation of John L. Lewis' Mine Workers, the intermittant affiliation of the Machinists, and the independence of the railway brotherhoods as examples. On the other hand, he warned, "If our union is split into warring camps by issues unrelated to wages and hours, you and your families will pay the price."

The AFL-CIO convention gave Cross one last chance to sway the Federation and it is a tribute to his rhetorical powers and ingenuity, as well as a testimony to the waste of his rare talent, that he garnered a good deal of sympathy from the convention with his speech. In the end, however, it was to be George Meany's day. "Yes, you heard a remarkable talk this afternoon," Meany's rebuttal began, "and this is a remarkable guy. But I have seen both sides of him, and I can tell you quite frankly that this Union is in a bad way if he continues to run its affairs. . . ." Meany went over Cross' misdeeds with a mastery of its details. "The effect of Cross' plea," the *Newark Evening News* reported, "was firmly erased by Meany who, for 45 minutes, spelled out the case against him with an indignation that more than matched that of Sen. McClellan after his select Senate committee drew out the story of Cross' expensive union leadership. . . ."

By a vote of 11,119,079 to 1,680,695, the Federation voted to expel the B&C, giving the AFL-CIO Executive Council authority to delay the effective date up to March 15 to give the Union time to reform itself in accordance with the Council's conditions. While some members of the Committee to Preserve Integrity who watched the proceedings from the gallery fretted at the possibility of a delay, Meany felt strongly that Cross would never step down and saw to it that the expulsion was effective immediately. For all practical purposes, the long connection of the B&C with the Federation was over on December 10, 1957.

"Organizing the unorganized. . . is won by hard work. It is done by day-to-day contact with these people, house visits, knocking on doors, getting insulted, standing outside of plants hand-billing. I know of no tougher or more time-consuming job than organizing, but at the same time I know of nothing more rewarding than when you can bring an unorganized group into the trade union movement and provide them with decent hours and working conditions." (John DeConcini, before the convention of the Pennsylvania State Board of the American Bakery and Confectionery Workers International Union, October 1962)

AFL-CIO President George Meany at the ABC's convention in Sept. 1958, with the former members of the Committee to Preserve Integrity. Left to Right: Curtis Sims, Daniel Conway, Meany, John DeConcini, Archie Goodman, and Amos Miller.

Years of the Split

What seemed like an ominous silence fell over Atlantic City. The AFL-CIO convention had disbanded. So had the convention of dissident bakers, delegates from 95 locals who had met concurrently to form an alternate body known as the American Bakery and Confectionery Workers International Union (ABC) and apply for a charter from the Federation. The ABC had elected the members of the Committee to Preserve Integrity as its temporary officers—Dan Conway, president; Curtis Sims, secretary-treasurer; John DeConcini, executive vice-president; Archie Goodman and Amos Miller, vice-presidents. They were becoming uncomfortable with what seemed like an unusual delay in receiving their charter from George Meany.

Finally Bill Schnitzler phoned to ask Conway and DeConcini to join him in his hotel room. Meany had decided to issue a charter to the ABC, Schnitzler informed them, but only on condition that Sims' name be dropped from the application. The reason, as far as Conway knew, was Meany's desire to prevent the division from being personified in the differences between Cross and Sims as individuals. Meany, in fact, still fumed over what he regarded as Sims' dilatoriness in bringing Cross' transgressions to light. In any case, after a conference with other members of the integrity committee, Conway reluctantly agreed to hold both acting positions himself, and the ABC became an AFL-CIO affiliate on December 12. To Meany's lasting enmity, however, Conway immediately appointed Sims as assistant to the president for financial affairs; there was a strong streak of stubborn righteousness in this new Bakers' leader. Sims became secretary-treasurer at the ABC convention in 1958.

What the new ABC faced in the months following the AFL-CIO convention was a whirlwind of activity on the part of Jim Cross, constantly on the offensive on all fronts. Immediately upon his return from Atlantic City, Cross established a special closed circuit telephone hookup so that he could directly address questions raised at B&C local meetings. On December 20, he communicated with all employers under contract with the B&C, warning them not to assist dissident elements in any way and cautioning that only B&C affiliates could participate in the Union's welfare and pension funds. At about the same time, he began distributing so-called "loyalty" postcards to members, by which a member could authorize the B&C to use his or her name in "any proceedings instituted for the protection of my contract rights and benefits or my Local's funds and properties." On January 11, the B&C General Executive Board officially expelled the five integrity committee members—Conway, Sims, DeConcini, Miller and Goodman—"for life," claiming preposterously that their activities amounted to a diversion of union funds from legitimate purposes, fostered dual unionism and were detrimental to the best interests of the membership. The Board did not even bother to hold a trial on the charges.

By the beginning of 1958, the B&C had tied up the funds of several locals that were attempting to disaffiliate. In a classic demonstration of carrot and stick tactics, Cross also announced that Segal and Co. was engaged in a survey with an eye to increasing B&C benefit levels. On the last day of March, the union trustees of the B&C welfare and pension funds informed the locals that they would discontinue benefits to any local that disaffiliated. Eleven days later, Cross announced that the B&C had instituted a $25,000 college scholarship fund.

If Cross' tactics allowed him to hold on to a core membership, it did not prevent the ABC from outstripping the B&C to become the leading union in the industry. Several factors lay behind the ABC's success. Conway and his associates proved to be creative and dedicated administrators. In the car leaving Atlantic City, Sims driving, Conway filled three writing tablets with outlines of what had to be done. Overnight, it seemed, they recreated a superstructure of governance and benefits for locals that joined the new organization. By January, the ABC had established a headquarters in

Washington, hired an office staff and organized a field staff. By April, an ABC Union and Industry Welfare Fund and Pension Fund were operating. In January, the ABC already had 60 locals and 44,800 members; in April, it had just about doubled that.

Daniel Conway

The ABC published the first issue of the *ABC News* in January. The new journal was temporarily under the editorship of AFL-CIO staff member John Harding; later in the year the ABC hired its own editor, experienced labor journalist Albert Herling, editor of the Washington, D.C., Central Labor Council's organ, the *Trade Unionist*. The Union distributed the *News* to ABC and B&C members alike, and its dependable and straightforward reporting increasingly became a source of confidence for ABC members while feeding B&C rank-and-file dissatisfaction with the administration of Jimmy Cross.

The ABC also developed a more democratic structure than the B&C, which was bound to prove a troublesome contrast to its competitor as well as a device for better meeting its members' needs. Instead of International officers dominating regional bargaining, the ABC required three of the five B&C participants to be local representatives. What is more, on the General Executive Board, the majority of the members were local union officers.

A series of major court victories helped wrench dissatisfied locals from Cross' stranglehold. With the advice of ABC General Counsel Henry Kaiser, lawyers for locals throughout the country argued that the schism in the B&C derived from the failure of its leadership to carry out its constitutional responsibility in good faith, as its expulsion from the AFL-CIO demonstrated, and this abrogated the contract between the B&C and its affiliates. The "schism principle" gained wide acceptance from the courts. On February 18, the 8,000-member Local 1 in Chicago sought to transfer to the ABC, and the B&C went to court seeking to place the local's headquarters and assets, worth approximately $200,000, under the trusteeship of Vice-President Russell Gamble. B&C supporters also tried unsuccessfully to physically take control of the local's headquarters. A few weeks later, the superior court of Cook County rendered a decision in the case of *Olson v. Carbonara*, so-named for new B&C secretary-treasurer, Peter H. Olson, and Local 1's acting president, Peter Carbonara. It ruled that the expulsion of the B&C from the AFL-CIO breached an "essential condition of the continued contractual relationship" between the B&C and its locals; this doctrine of "frustration of contract" ended Local 1's obligations under the B&C constitution.

Over the next year, courts throughout the country sustained the ABC in a series of precedent-setting cases. In early March, the superior court in San Francisco blocked the attempt of the B&C to seize the assets of Local 24. "There is nothing whatsoever in this record to indicate or hint that the defendants, officers of the new local, are anything but men of honor and integrity," the court noted. "No shadow has been cast upon them as has been cast by certain records on the officers of the old expelled international." A month later, the Milwaukee circuit court ordered five baking companies to turn over dues checkoffs to ABC Local 205, proclaiming that although the local had withdrawn from the B&C in January, it was the "continuing entity" of B&C Local 205. In May, the circuit court in Jackson County, Missouri, blocked the discharge of eight Kansas City bakers, four at A&P and four at Safeway. The firms had tried to fire them because they switched from the B&C to the ABC.

During the remainder of the year, cases built upon these early precedents crimped Cross' efforts across the country to lock in dissatisfied locals. By the early spring, Cross watched the ABC move into the leading position. True, the B&C health and welfare and pension funds still controlled the cumulative past contributions of the members; a suit by the ABC languished in the courts for 20 months before an out-of-court settlement in July 1960 turned over a quarter of a million dollars to the ABC funds. Even this was a small fraction of the $3 million the ABC sought. Nevertheless, as soon as the *ABC News* began publicizing the issuance of the ABC's first benefits checks in the spring of 1958, Cross' loss-of-benefits issue began to lose some of its credibility.

By April 1958, the existence of 120 ABC locals representing 75,000 members convincingly demonstrated the erosion of Cross' base. With an ABC national A&P council coordinating the efforts of 14 A&P locals and an ABC Northeastern Seaboard Conference—first of a projected network of regional conferences—drafting bargaining goals for the summer's negotiations, the ABC was quickly reducing Cross' efforts to a defensive holding action.

This growth resulted not only from solid legal defense and effective administration but also from an enormous effort in the field. George Meany provided Federation support in the form of a $50,000 loan and total financial assistance estimated as high as $100,000 by Roscoe Born of the *Wall Street Journal*. Born also noted that individual unions made further loans to the new Bakers' union. In addition,

Meany instructed AFL-CIO organizers throughout the country to focus their attention on getting the ABC started. This support provided the underpinning for the initial spate of "spontaneous revolts" in many locals. William Kircher, the AFL-CIO's assistant regional director in Cincinnati, became a "one man gang," DeConcini recalled, "leading all the B&C members in the city of Cincinnati out of the B&C and into the ABC." Kircher's activities extended to other Midwestern cities as well, such as Columbus and Cleveland.

Basically, however, it was unrelenting road work by the bakers themselves that created the momentum for the new organization, and no one carried more of the weight of the road campaign than John DeConcini. DeConcini's grandfather, father and several uncles had been active in the United Mine Workers of America in the Pennsylvania coal fields, and three months after DeConcini found work at General Baking Company in Philadelphia in 1937 at the age of 19, he was active in the campaign to organize his shop. A shop steward before his first year was out, he was elected president of Local 6 in 1940. Wes Reedy tapped him as a fulltime organizer for the local in March 1941. Seven months later, DeConcini joined the armed services, attending officers' training school and serving as a first lieutenant in the Paratroop's 11th Airborne Division in the Phillipines, Okinawa and Japan. After the war, DeConcini served as organizer, business agent and president of his local before becoming an International representative in 1952 and International vice-president at the very end of that year.

Before the split, DeConcini had made a reputation for himself as a tough, self-assured and respected leader. Wes Reedy offered him a chance to join the AFL-CIO staff, reasoning that anyone closely associated with Bill Schnitzler, as DeConcini was, would be in a difficult position remaining in the B&C under Cross. DeConcini decided to stay with the B&C, however, determined to see the storm through.

Soon DeConcini was able to catalogue a growing list of personal confrontations between himself and the B&C president. At lunch break at the July 1956 board meeting, Cross tried unsuccessfully to gain his support to place $50,000 in a president's discretionary fund, DeConcini insisting on accountability in all expenditures. Following the 1956 San Francisco convention, DeConcini personally warned Cross that the day of reckoning was coming if he failed to clean up his act. Subsequently, Cross offered DeConcini the position of director of organization if he would stay with the B&C rather than joining the effort to form a new bakers' union. The offer was proferred through James Landriscina, who had always claimed that he controlled DeConcini because they both were Italian; DeConcini's rejection cleared up that final illusion.

Earl Tetrick, former business agent of Terre Haute Local 70 and a B&C International representative from 1956, later recalled that there was a general feeling in the B&C at the time of the split that the ABC simply could not succeed. The lessons of past schisms were ingrained in many bakers' minds, and loyalty to the old International ran deep. There was also a tradition of local autonomy and independent mindedness in the B&C, however, and DeConcini's savvy and inexhaustible energy in particular mobilized this tradition on the ABC's behalf. Donald Fink, one of DeConcini's early recruits for the ABC field staff, recalled that "John was every place, I don't know how...the man was tireless," both the "most convincing speaker you ever heard in your life" and the "most active man that I ever met in my life in the labor movement."

In his efforts, DeConcini built up a corps of local leaders, men who, he remembered, "laid their jobs on the line to switch their organizations into the ABC." In each section, certain key individuals emerged to "carry the ball." In New York, he had Louis Genuth in Local 50, Nathan Erhlich and Harry Lorber in Local 51, and Joe Kane in Local 525. Charles McCluskey played a similar role in Washington, D.C. There was a formidable phalanx across the Midwest made up of such individuals as Jerry Froehlig in Minneapolis, Russell Prince in Joplin, Missouri, Pete Carbonara in Chicago, Billy Meyers in Kansas City, Howard Callahue in St. Louis and Maurice Liesen in Quincy, Illinois. The B&C remained strong in the West, where the locals tended to stick together and work for reform from within. In California, nevertheless, San Francisco leaders Ed Kemmitt of Local 24 and Austin Tulley of candy workers Local 158, and Virgil Cummings from Oakland Local 125, gave the ABC a hold on what was patently B&C country. Meanwhile, in the South, Curtis Sims and Amos Miller gained the ABC the support of practically every local leader in the fourth region.

The ABC not only won over the locals with which its leaders had close ties but in many cases successfully appealed to shop stewards working under hostile leaders to rise and fight against local officers sympathetic with the B&C. This especially strengthed the ABC's showing in the biscuit and cracker industry and the bakery and grocery chains. Kenneth McLellan was a shop steward in New England for A&P who led his local into the ABC. In Pittsburgh, Pat D'Angelo of Nabisco along with Attilio Mascaro of Liberty Baking Company led the fight against local officers who chose to remain in the B&C. About two-thirds of the members joined them in switching affiliation. D'Angelo and Mascaro went on to become top leaders of the national organization in the subsequent decades.

In the end, the B&C held on to less than two-fifths of its membership. Many of those who stayed with the B&C believed that the most effective way to deal with the B&C's crisis was to work for reform from the inside. The special convention of the B&C in Cincinnati, March 3-5, 1958, directed its leaders to work for a reunification with the ABC and seemed to encourage Cross' resignation by urging that "whatever may be the justified self-interest of any one individual be subordinated to the ultimate welfare of the entire membership."

Other groups in the B&C, however, felt that any settlement requiring Cross' ouster would be dishonorable, some preferring to remain independent and others to seek affiliation with the Teamsters instead. In fact, if Cross had an ace in the hole following the split, it was his long connection with Jimmy Hoffa, their friendship going back to their youth in Detroit. It was obvious from the spotlight Hoffa enjoyed at the B&C convention that Cross hoped either to frighten the ABC and the AFL-CIO into a compromise reunion or to lead the bakers into Hoffa's organization in short order. Since the convention provided that the B&C should take no action toward reunion that was in conflict with the B&C constitution, Cross seemed to have a free hand to reject any proposal that required him to resign.

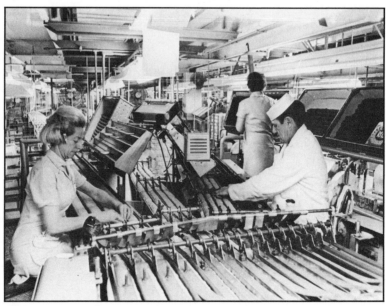

Cracker packaging at Nabisco, 1960. Courtesy, Nabisco Brands.

In May 1959, Hoffa announced in a *New York Times* interview that four-man committees of his union and the B&C had been meeting on the question of merging and that the talks were so far along that the arrangements had been turned over to the lawyers. The announcement caused a revolt in B&C ranks. Local 3 of New York, with the cooperation of the B&C Pacific Coast Conference, led a movement for reaffiliation with the ABC. Cross, in turn, sought to mollify the insurgents by appointing a B&C reunification committee consisting of board members Robert Hart, Henry Bartosh, Max Kralstein, John Reid and Gean Triplett. The committee proved unwilling, however, to seek reunion on any but Cross' terms. During July, it communicated with George Meany, asking him to agree to reunification through negotiations rather than on the basis of the AFL-CIO Executive Council's directives. When Meany refused, the committee held meetings with rank-and-file members in seven cities and claimed that each meeting endorsed the committee's insistence upon a negotiated and "honorable settlement," one which apparently involved retaining the B&C's officers in any merged body.

Local 3 accused the committee of distorting the membership meetings, claiming that at one meeting in New York, representatives of 20,000 members were prepared to propose a resolution calling for Cross' immediate retirement; the representatives agreed to withhold the resolution only after the reunification committee appealed to them on the basis of tactical considerations. At a meeting in Oakland representing 14,000 members, it revealed, such a resolution reached the floor before a similar request by the committee sidetracked it.

Local 3, together with Los Angeles Local 37, now called representatives of B&C locals to meet in St. Louis in November 1959 to take action on reunification. There, representatives of 15 locals established the Local Unions Reunification Committee, consisting of Skeets Moschetta, Frank Dutto, Albert Meyer, Charlie Landers, and Walter Friese. On January 8, this committee met with Cross in Washington, D.C. Cross insisted that he would not only not retire but had arranged to hold the next B&C national convention in Detroit in October 1962, at which time he intended to seek reelection. B&C Vice-President Henry Alvino, one of the Board members who objected to these arrangements, lost his $11,250-a-year position as an International representative.

On March 8, 1960, the Local Unions Reunification Committee instructed its attorney to file suit against Cross and Pete Olson in Washington, D.C., District Court, on the basis of misappropriations of union funds. These included heavy attorneys' fees related to

Cross' appearance before the AFL-CIO Ethical Practices Committee, his testimony at the McClellan hearings and his perjury trial resulting from it, and his February 1959 trial on embezzlement arising from his relationship with George Stuart. Stuart was sentenced to a term in prison in February 1959 for embezzling funds of Chicago locals that he supervised as a trustee. The case against Cross ended in a directed acquittal for lack of direct evidence tying Cross to Stuart's activities in Chicago at the time. After the trial, the Reunification Committee's suit contended, Cross began making payments to Stuart's wife from the B&C treasury, payments that were still continuing. In addition, the suit claimed that the B&C had paid $65,000 to maintain Cross' personal residences in Palm Beach and at the Dupont Plaza and Woodner Hotels, plus paying his personal bills for food, telephone, automobile, entertainment and trips by Mrs. Cross.

The committee also went to court to stop Cross from punishing officers active in the reunification campaign or the suit against him. In addition to Alvino, Cross in June dismissed Max Kralstein, George Siebold and Peter Sullivan from their jobs as International representatives. He scheduled trials for Alvino and Kralstein. In August, however, in the first test of Section 609 of the Landrum-Griffin Act, the U.S. District Court in Washington, D.C., ruled that the actions had been retaliatory, reinstated the officers with back pay, and provided that there could be no further proceedings against Alvino and Kralstein or reprisals against others supporting the suit against Cross.

Faced with impending judicial scrutiny of the B&C accounts under his tenure, Cross finally decided to negotiate a settlement with the Reunification Committee. On January 26, 1961, Pete Olson reported to the B&C on the conclusion of an agreement under which Cross would retire with a lump-sum settlement of his pension rights in the amount of $250,000 in cash, and the committee would discontinue its court action against the B&C. Pending federal court approval of the agreement, Cross went on a leave of absence and a three-man committee consisting of Olson, as chairman, and Kralstein and Landriscina, took over the president's duties.

In the meantime, however, newly-appointed Secretary of Labor Arthur Goldberg immediately moved to have the Bureau of Labor Management Reports undertake a full investigation of the agreement to see whether it violated any federal law. What the Bureau uncovered marked the final undoing of Jim Cross and his closest collaborators. The 1960 B&C report to the Bureau included an expenditure of $35,000 entered as a refund to New York Local 3 of a strike donation. Officials of Local 3, however, denied ever receiving this money. The cancelled check had been made out to Peter H. Olson as "payee of Local 3." When compliance officers questioned them about this payment, both Cross and Olson stated that the money had been placed in safe keeping for the local because of the possibility that dissidents in the local might tie up the funds. B&C records for the period between January and March 1960, however, showed that the B&C had issued large checks in round numbers to various union vice-presidents and International representatives, checks that totalled about $35,000. A Boston attorney for two of these individuals indicated that their clients had been asked to cash the checks, file false statements on how the money was spent, and then return the cash to union headquarters. The evidence was turned over to a federal grand jury.

These revelations forced the B&C General Executive Board to suspend Cross and Olson in March 1961. The Board named Max Kralstein acting secretary-treasurer. It awarded Cross a pension of about $1,100 a month, the money to accumulate, however, as equity pledged against any amount Cross might be found to owe the Union.

It proved difficult, however, for the B&C to shake Cross' legacy. Despite the fact that Jim Landriscina and Lester Crawford were among the Board members who the Labor Department revealed had participated in the Cross kick-back scheme, their supporters on the Board in May 1961 appointed Landriscina as president and Lester Crawford as secretary-treasurer. Landriscina invited Jimmy Hoffa to the General Executive Board in September and in other ways sought to prepare the way for a B&C-Teamsters merger. But in a court-ordered B&C convention in Cleveland in January 1962, the Union turned away both Hoffa and Landriscina.

The Cleveland convention considered the question of merging with another organization, but the debate was confusing and prolonged due to the introduction of three resolutions on the subject. The first called for merger with the ABC, but on such conditions as the AFL-CIO might dictate; its distasteful wording led to its defeat. But if the supporters of a Teamsters' merger thought this would pave the way for their resolution, they soon watched a roll call vote decisively turn them down. The convention also rejected a third merger proposal that favored maintaining the B&C as an independent organization. The B&C in effect remained on record, therefore, as favoring reunification.

What is more, the results of the election of officers seemed to promise a speedy reconciliation of the two organizations. The pro-Teamsters faction nominated Harvey Friedman for president; he lost

The Solar Building.

by a margin of almost two to one to Max Kralstein. A similar margin elected Henry Bartosh over Friedman's running mate, Lester Crawford. Joining Kralstein and Bartosh was a new General Executive Board dominated by Local Unions Reunification Committee candidates. The convention created a seven-member reunification committee consisting of four representatives of the rank and file and three Board members.

Kralstein instituted a general policy of streamlining the B&C's administration to cope with the effects of Cross' years of financial excess. The new president slashed his own salary from $30,000 to $20,000, including expenses. In the Solar Building, which the B&C had purchased and occupied as its headquarters since May 1958, he cut back the space the Union occupied by one-third, renting out the remainder. He also reduced the size of the staff. These cutbacks stood in stark contrast to the ABC which, holding its 1962 convention in Washington, D.C., just across the street from the Solar Building, demonstrated its robust health by voting to increase its per capita tax.

Soon after the general house-cleaning in the B&C, the saga of Jimmy Cross and his cohorts came to a dismal end. In March, a federal grand jury indicted Pete Olson for stealing, embezzlement and false bookkeeping. Olson decided to cooperate with investigators and was allowed to plead guilty to a lesser count. He revealed that Cross had asked for his help and that of other Board members in

1959 to put together the $35,000 Cross felt he needed to rig the jury in his favor in his trial for perjury. Cross, Olson testified, told him to follow Jim Landriscina's instructions on the disposition of the money. On February 13, 1959, therefore, Olson met Landriscina and a stranger on the street and turned over the money to them. Olson also confessed to later suggesting to Cross that he find a way to put the $35,000 back in the treasury before it was discovered by the auditors, the suggestion that eventually led to Cross' plan to have his supporters falsify expense accounts and kick back money to cover the shortage.

On examination, Landriscina identified the stranger as attorney Milton Levin, the man who later became B&C general counsel when Landriscina assumed the B&C presidency. Landriscina admitted to having gone to Levin to ask his help in fixing Cross' perjury trial. Levin agreed to take care of the trial for $35,000. Evidence later showed that Levin simply pocketed the money and never approached anyone concerning the fix. He nevertheless claimed to have accomplished what he promised when the trial ended in a directed acquittal.

As a result of the investigation, Cross was convicted of embezzlement and attempting to fix his trial, receiving a one- to three-year sentence on each of four counts, to run concurrently. Of the other B&C officers involved in the scheme, Pete Olson received four years on probation and James Landriscina was fined $2,500. Lester Crawford received one to three years, with the stipulation that the first six months be in prison with the rest suspended to be served on probation. Frank Mykalo and Frank Gardone received one- to three-year suspended sentences.

Max Kralstein

In Max Kralstein, the B&C had acquired an irrascible, ambitious and excitable president. At 63, Kralstein already had a long career behind him, one that saw him take the instrumental role in effecting a series of mergers of New York City locals; the capstone of this activity was the uniting of Locals 1, 3, 17, 164, 288 and 579 to construct the modern Local 3 in 1955. He left a similar legacy in the surrounding cities of Trenton, Newark, Paterson and Passaic. Many on the new B&C Board thought that Kralstein's presidency would now be a short one, paving the way for the long-awaited reunification with the ABC, a fitting finale considering his long track record.

The six years' delay in achieving reunification were a tribute to a residue of bad feeling, an incorrigibleness of personality and underlying personal ambition that all affected key individuals' vision at crucial intervals. Fourteen months of intermittant meetings between ABC and B&C reunification committees and between the respective presidents of the two organizations culminated in the unsuccessful effort of George Meany to mediate a merger agreement. The difficulty appeared to lie in the ABC's desire to weight the leadership of the new organization in its favor, because of its preponderance of membership, a position which Meany accepted in the plan he presented at the end of April 1963. By Meany's plan, the ABC would nominate the president and the treasurer of the unified organization, the B&C the financial secretary, with each organization nominating one executive vice-president and nine vice-presidents.

It took Kralstein's own peculiar brand of stubbornness to ignore the inevitable dominance of the ABC, considering that its members outnumbered the B&C's approximately two to one. On the other side, Dan Conway was bearing his own cross during these years which did not make compromise any easier. He perceived that what Kralstein was most interested in was preserving the position of secretary-treasurer and occupying that position himself in any merged organization. The secretary-treasurership, though, was Curtis Sims' job, and Conway in all these years never flagged in his determination to demonstrate his loyalty to Sims. To Conway, satisfying Kralstein always boiled down to "giving away Sims' job."

In 1968, Kralstein became the third B&C president to look to the Teamsters for his salvation, leading his organization into affiliation with that union which was now led by Frank Fitzsimmons. Vice-President Gregory Oskoian, the former business agent and financial secretary of Local 447 in Providence, Rhode Island, first explored the idea with Teamsters officials, and a special B&C convention in April 1968 approved the arrangement. In return for paying the Teamsters a monthly per capita tax of 5 cents, the B&C gained the promise of mutual protection against raiding, mutual assistance in contract negotiations and a guarantee of complete independence and autonomy. As Earl Tetrick later reminisced, the B&C board was well aware of the potential psychological effect the arrangement might have on the ABC.

As a means of overcoming the B&C's apparent isolation, the arrangement made sense to many members of the B&C Board. Before the first year was out, however, there were widespread rumors that a full merger was in the making, one that would create an autonomous bakery workers' division in the Teamsters headed by Kralstein and Oskoian. Albert Meyer, vice-president out of Los Angeles Local 37 and a former Local Unions Reunification Committee activist, recalled confronting both Kralstein and Oskoian over the issue at the time they were all together for one of their periodic meetings with Fitzsimmons. According to Meyer, Kralstein tried to bring up the issue of a full merger during the meeting, at which point Meyer suggested they break for lunch. By the time lunch was over, Meyer was convinced that Kralstein, and not Oskoian, was behind the merger idea, and he made it clear that he would oppose it. The meeting with Fitzsimmons never reconvened and the B&C ceased paying its per capita tax to the Teamsters at that point.

Kralstein's interest in the Teamsters may well have been his reaction to growing indications that he would not be able to retain the B&C presidency for another term. Henry Alvino later claimed that Kralstein and he originally had agreed that Kralstein would only serve as president for one year and then retire. When the year was out, Alvino contended, Kralstein threatened to pull his local out of the B&C if he were removed, while promising to energetically pursue merger if he remained in office. As at many times in his career, Kralstein's bullying style apparently worked for him but contributed to a general disaffection that grew over time.

Having subsequently failed to bring about a merger with the ABC and, in fact, suffering since the middle of the decade a general intensification of competitive raiding from the ABC, Kralstein tested the waters on the Teamsters issue. There were significant pockets of interest in a merger with the Teamsters by the late 1960s, particularly among locals in the West. Somewhere along the line, however, Kralstein decided that the Teamsters' sentiment was not strong enough, or that those whose supported a merger with the Teamsters were not equally enthusiastic about him.

In the early summer of 1969, therefore, Kralstein sought out Wesley Reedy, who enjoyed the respect of the leaders of both the B&C and the ABC, and asked him to help bring the two organizations together. By August, meetings between Kralstein, Conway and Reedy had concluded a no-raiding agreement and were developing the details of a merger plan between the ABC and the B&C. Reedy set up a panel consisting of Lane Kirkland, who became AFL-CIO secretary-treasurer on Bill Schnitzler's retirement in 1969, and mediators Theodore Kheel and David Cole; the three stood willing to solve outstanding problems as a last resort.

At the same time, a last roadblock to merger within the ABC disappeared with the resignation of Curtis Sims in August. Sims had been resisting merger on the grounds that the plan that was developing called for the B&C to nominate the secretary-treasurer of the merged organization. An issue extraneous to the merger negotiations arose, however, when Conway asked Sims to adopt a new computer system for the ABC, and Sims resisted. When Conway assigned John DeConcini to install the system, Sims offered his resignation. Conway decided to accept it. DeConcini held the secretary-treasurership on an interim basis, strongly committed as he was to filling it with a B&C nominee to facilitate the merger.

In the course of the negotiations, real statesmanship emerged. Often during the discussions, Reedy recollected, Conway and Kralstein seemed determined to iron out difficult issues rather than see them handed to the impartial panel for resolution. Often one or the other would say "Hell we're going to settle this problem ourselves, we're not going to let a panel decide this problem, which is our resposibility." To Reedy, it was a touching end to a tumultuous era: "At long last, personal pride became an integral part of merger discussions."

In December, the two organizations merged, retaining the older name of the Bakery and Confectionery Workers' International Union and the connection with the long traditions it represented. What had emerged from 12 years of division was a Union that was more democratic than ever, and one that united the best elements of the B&C and the ABC.

9,000 ABC members at 13 Nabisco plants began a successful 56-day strike on Sept. 7, 1969 to assure that their wages kept up with spiraling inflation.

Epilogue

Rebirth

"We have more reasons for becoming involved politically than ever before in the history of the labor movement....We want to see arbitrary plant closings stopped; we want to see the end of concession bargaining; we want to see the end of union busting; we want to see the end of exporting jobs abroad by conglomerates; we want to see the end of high unemployment and high interest rates; we want to see all Americans with an opportunity to work and earn a decent wage; we want to see a government that will spend more time negotiating for peace rather than preparing for war." (John DeConcini, message in BC&T News, *February 1984)*

I n some ways, great events like the merger distract the eye from more fundamental trends and turning points that control the destiny of people and movements. In essence, the one great issue that divided the B&C in 1957 was practically settled in 1958 when the ABC codified a basic moral order of accountability in its new constitution. It limited the amount of funds the secretary-treasurer of the International and its locals could possess at any time, required monthly financial statements from every local, limited convention expense allowances, provided for the immediate auditing of the accounts of officers who were not reelected, and limited to a minority the number of Board members who could be regular salaried members of the ABC staff.

The ABC strictly controlled the use of trusteeships to govern troubled local unions, establishing a 20-member panel elected by the ABC annual conventions to oversee the institution. To impose a trusteeship, the president would first have to garner approval of two-thirds of the General Executive Board, then submit the proposal to a three-member committee selected by the chairperson of the trusteeship panel from among its members. None of the three could come from the geographical area of the local involved. If this committee approved, a trusteeship could be imposed, but for no longer than six months without the convening of a new hearing to grant an extension.

A modern worker with a display of production line baked goods. Courtesy, General Foods.

A modern cake decorator.

The history of the two organizations thereafter was a painful and drawnout denouement as the B&C relieved itself of the burdens of Jim Cross' leadership and the B&C and ABC leaders overcame the legacy of self-defeating division that most knew in the end could not go on indefinitely. The greatest costs were the enormous legal fees involved in contending for jurisdiction, lost opportunities for cooperating to establish regional patterns and a solid front in negotiations with employers, and the diversion of resources that could have been used to organize the unorganized. In 1974, when the delegates gathered for the second convention of the merged organization—designated as the 29th convention to assert a continuity with the B&C past—40 to 50 percent of the workers in the Union's jurisdiction remained unorganized.

Now the B&C was forced to try to make up lost ground in a time of mounting unemployment and runaway inflation. During the mid-1970s, the baking industry was staggered first by the runaway cost of flour, followed by a general increase in everything from sugar and shortening to paper products and natural gas. National economic policy complicated these problems as the baking industry felt the inflationary implications of the United States' wheat deal with the Soviet Union and deregulation of natural gas, while macaroni and candy workers faced increased competition from imported products.

Intensifying the problem of organizing was a general decline in the number of jobs in the B&C's jurisdiction due to automation. By 1970, most members of the Union worked in highly mechanized workplaces, whether producing bread and cake, biscuits and crackers, candy, macaroni, potato chips or pretzels. Within their lifetimes, the older members had watched machines encroaching on hand work. Al Meyer, for instance, remembered that many bakers in the West Coast shops he was most familiar with still worked by hand at their benches at the time of World War II. During the 1950s, however, only the manufacturers of specialty-type breads remained insulated from automation. By the early 1960s, the rest were well on their way to continuous-flow operations and the modern integrated assembly line.

In the face of the need for modern, systematic approaches to revolutionary changes in the workplace, the leaders of the B&C seemed anxious to bury the personal differences of the past as quickly as possible. From the first Board meeting, Dan Conway related in 1974, "we never made a decision except. . . in unanimous agreement. Previous affiliation never entered any discussion or affected any decision." Contributing to the reconciliation was the fact that an increasing number of Board members had entered the Union's leadership after the split, while a growing number of the principals in the old disputes left the scene through retirement or death. Max Kralstein retired in 1970 after a dispute involving his unauthorized decision to provide Attorney Herman Cooper with a substantial payment in recognition of past services. Gregory Oskoian replaced Kralstein as secretary-treasurer. B&C old-timers Charlie Aumiller, born at the turn of the century, and Hugo Neuffer, a few years his senior and an immigrant from Germany, died in 1972 and 1973, respectively. In February 1974, the *B&C News* announced the deaths of both Kralstein and Harvey Friedman. Three months later it reported the retirement of John Reid, long-time Canadian mainstay on the B&C Board.

As the divisions of the past faded they were covered over by closely coordinated regional bargaining activities that created a new sense of common goals and common experience. Not only did this strategic coordination enable members to keep up with spiraling inflation in terms of wages as well as employer contributions to the welfare and pension plans, but cooperation between the third region, representing the Southern states, and the fourth region, representing the Midwest, finally brought the South up to national standards. For Willie Cullins, an International representatives from Jacksonville, the achievement capped a lifelong fight against discrimination that he had experienced doubly as a Southerner and as a black man.

At the time Cullins got his first job at A&P in Jacksonville in 1941, a black man in the South could find work in the industry only as a utility man—working sanitation, handling and receiving—or at the oven. He started at 35 cents an hour. Oven men made 45 cents; utility men, 55. The top-paying jobs as mixers were off limits to blacks. Cullins well remembered how the company often used him to train young white men who in short order became his supervisors: "These guys would come in off the farm." he related, "they was working around the plant, the superintendent would put them with me.... The next thing this fellow was tellin' me what to do." That, he said, was when he decided to join the Union.

In his early years, he was one of the few blacks in the Union, and the annual contracts that generally awarded a nickel raise for production workers at the same time tended to give the sanitation jobs in which blacks were concentrated a paltry 2 cents. "I could remember being the only black at meetings," Cullins said, thinking back to 1945. He told fellow blacks: "you'll never get more than two cents if you don't participate." He himself moved from being the steward for the oven men, all of whom were black at the time, to a place on the local's negotiating committee and executive board in the 1950s. Halfway through the decade, Amos Miller began asking him to go on out-of-town organizing trips for the International. There was little integration in the shops until the civil rights movement and the Civil Rights Act of the early 1960s, but in 1964, Cullins was asked to join the International staff. From then on he organized throughout the South, often precarious and intimidating work where hostility, whippings and worse were always a possibility from those who felt threatened by interracial unionism.

Cullins and International Representative Fred Chester led the team that conducted the campaign in the mid-1970s to organize Russell Stover, one of the largest candy manufacturers in the country. ABC Local 218 in Kansas City signed the first Russell Stover contract in 1967. It did not augur well for the future that negotiations, conducted by a team headed by Board members John DeConcini and Russell Prince, took 32 bargaining sessions and nine months from the time the NLRB certified the local as the representative of 450 Stover workers. In June 1974 the B&C lost an election at Russell Stover's Montrose, Colorado, plant, by a vote of 133 to 101. Seventeen months later, however, the NLRB ordered a new election after finding that the employer had engaged in widespread acts of intimidation such as interrogation during preemployment interviews concerning prospective employees' views on unions, threatening to close the plant if the employees chose to unionize, and withholding wage increases granted to employees at other Russell Stover plants because of the Union's campaign at Montrose.

In the meantime, in November 1974, the B&C won an election at another Russell Stover plant, workers in Lincoln, Nebraska, giving 392 votes to the B&C as compared to 216 to "no union." "Every possible anti-union ploy was used," the *B&C News* reported, "with a constant barrage of anti-union propanganda plastered on so-called 'truth boards' spread around the plant." Following the election, the company immediately filed unfair practices charges against the B&C designed, the Union's representatives felt, simply to delay the certification date and the onset of negotiations for a first contract. In April, the NLRB's regional director found Stover's charges unfounded and without merit; the company then filed an appeal with the NLRB in Washington. It was not, therefore, until September 1975, a full year after the certification vote, that negotiations got underway in Lincoln.

The course of the Russell Stover struggle emphasized the nationwide interdependency of local unions and the growing need of coordination and leadership from the International. In February 1976, the B&C launched a national boycott of Russell Stover products, suported by the AFL-CIO. As consumer picket lines went up across the country, the B&C petitioned for representation elections at other Russell Stover operations.

In June 1976, workers at the Stover plant in Marion, South Carolina, voted 410 to 177 for the B&C. During this campaign, the company distributed anti-union propaganda—including a personal letter from company Board Chairman Louis L. Ward which blamed unions for the plant closings—and showed an anti-union film that attributed violence to unions. Behind the campaign in South Carolina, which also included a 13-to-1 B&C victory at Ward's paper box company, lay some solid groundwork by International Representatives Fred Chester and Willie Cullins in the local communities, so that company workers from Florence, Marion, Latta, Dillon and Gresham faced the crisis with support and encouragement from their neighbors. The International also filed a class action suit in the United States District Court in Charleston charging that the 85 percent of its workers who were black were excluded from supervisory jobs as well as other key jobs in maintenance and on the office and clerical staff.

In October 1976, the B&C and the company ended their struggle in the offices of the Federal Mediation and Conciliation Service by signing a 29½ month contract for the company's Lincoln plant and establishing a framework for settlements at other locations. Part of the agreement involved setting aside outstanding suits and settling the issues they involved through negotiation. Thus the Marion agreement a month later included a non-discrimination clause as well as providing for the reinstatement with back pay of 15 union activitists the company had fired.

The maturation of regional bargaining and national coordination of company-wide campaigns changed the relationship between national leadership and the membership on the local level. It was to this extent a sign of the times that in March 1978, after some hesitation, Dan Conway decided to step down from the B&C presidency in favor of the man who most epitomized a national leader in touch with the rank and file. Conway had given the ABC and the reunited B&C a long term of stability under a distinguished and intelligent administration. His presence and his unimpugned integrity had also made the symbolic and cermonial functions he performed as presiding officer in the Union's internal gatherings as well as in representing the B&C in the International Union of Food and Allied Workers a source of real strength for the organization. The Union now made way for a man who, in his extensive road experience, had developed a sixth sense of how to knit the rank and file and the International leadership into a modern working organization.

John DeConcini

At the very time that John DeConcini was assuming office, the 137,000-member B&C was discussing the possibilities of merger with the Tobacco Workers International Union, a union of 30,000 whose philosophy was grounded on a belief that close coordination and communication with the rank and file was essential to effective leadership. René Rondou, a Canadian of Belgian descent, had built his career on a tight-knit relationship with his locals. By the time he became president of the TWIU, the Canadian locals had shaken loose from a reputation as the weak sisters of the organization to become equal and in some respects leading partners with the more numerous locals in the States.

If the basic products of the two unions were different, many points naturally linked the two. Baked goods and tobacco products shared many of the same distribution points through the grocery industry. Tobacco corporations, in their efforts to diversify, were expanding into the food industry, bringing more and more members of the B&C and the TWIU under common employers. The members of both organizations, furthermore, were by and large facing common problems of automation, plant closings and the evolution of their emloyers into multi-national giants.

The merger convention in August 1978 changed the name of the organization to the Bakery, Confectionery and Tobacco Workers International Union. The tobacco workers gave the organization added strength in the South and Canada, while bringing the number of women in the combined organization to more than 40,000, and adding fresh blood to the leadership. René Rondou became executive vice-president of the BC&T. When Secretary-Treasurer Gregory Oskoian died unexpectedly of a heart attack shortly after the convention, the organization elevated Rondou to the number two post. The two leaders, DeConcini reflected in 1982, "became closer each day and each day it seems that we were never apart."

Symbolizing the strength of the merged body was its new headquarters. After the B&C and ABC merged in 1969, the organization sold the B&C's Solar Building and put the proceeds into a building fund. It was not until August 1980, however, that the Union dedicated its new building in the Washington suburb of Kensington, Maryland. The Health and Welfare and Pension Funds, for decades a bedrock of the members' security, occupied the first three floors, a fitting base for the Union's administrative headquarters on the top floor.

In the years that followed the 1978 convention, the character of the BC&T changed significantly; it became self-consciously innovative, militant and progressive across the entire range of its activities. One distinctive aspect of DeConcini's leadership had always been his commitment to political action. His involvement in the activities of the AFL-CIO Committee on Political Action in the early 1970s

BC&T headquarters, Kensington, Maryland.

led the way for the organization, and the year he assumed the presidency of the BC&T, the convention established its own political action committee, BCT-PAC. The establishment of the committee represented only the beginning of his effort to educate the members in "the political realities of life," the increasing sophistication with which employers and their lawyers were able to neutralize workers' basic guarantees under the National Labor Relations Act and other legislation, and the political effectiveness of the right wing in beating back labor law reform. As he bluntly laid it out at the 1978 convention, "Deep in the hearts of corporate management, they'd like to get rid of us."

To DeConcini, a union had to be a mobilized organization or it was nothing at all. "If you're going to vote for this proposal," he said of BCT-PAC, "and then go home and do nothing, I'd rather you vote against it." He fully intended to see that in political action, as well as in organizing and effective representation of the workers, the locals themselves became the militant front line of the BC&T's forces.

In all of these areas, the code word for DeConcini's initiative was "education." In the spring of 1979, the BC&T inaugurated its first area educational conferences for local union officers and stewards in order to begin converting the mass of apparently apathetic members into activists, "organizing the organized," DeConcini called it. Conference sessions provided simulated organizing experience, reviewed the requirements of the Occupational Safety and Health Act and the Landrum-Griffin Act, and went over basic BC&T internal procedures for obtaining permission to strike. They also exposed these local leaders to the basic philosophy of the leadership through upbeat explanations of the importance of registering members to vote and educating them to vote according to their interests, involving women more centrally in local union governance and activities, and alerting members to the onslaught of union-busting accompanying rising right-wing sentiment in the country.

The following year, the International expanded its educational activities, calling its first national educational conference. For the five-day conference in Washington, August 17 to 22, locals were allowed to send up to eight delegates. The 400 participants from 100 locals went through a range of sessions from political talks by key politicians, to collective bargaining workshops, to a showing of the film "Norma Rae." The International held a separate smaller conference shortly afterwards for Canadian locals.

Through the core of the program ran certain deep concerns. During the first six months of 1980, the BC&T lost more members than it organized. It lost more NLRB elections than it won. Only 26 locals, 12 percent of the total, participated in any type of organizing activity. What is more, as had been true in the early 1970s when 50 percent of the International's members voted for Richard Nixon, it was apparent that Ronald Reagan was making significant inroads in convincing workers that he shared their concerns. Reagan, Board members explained to the conference, "has consistently been against the issues that organized labor supports and as a result has the support of anti-labor groups."

Educational programs continued to expand throughout the early 1980s; indeed the process of communicating with the members emerged as the linchpin of the organization, the single most important objective in the Union's agenda. In the summer of 1981, the International inaugurated a series of regional summer educational conferences. At the 1982 convention in Hollywood, Florida, it established a program to pay a portion of the costs of sending delegates

171

Lane Kirkland and John DeConcini.

to conferences: its objective was to make it possible for more than just the principal officers of local unions to attend, bringing in the shop-level leaders who would be the cadres of the organization. The intensity behind the proposal was apparent in DeConcini's explanation to the delegates: "This will permit this union to have a cadre of 2,000 to 3,000 additional activists who will become politically active, who will assist in organizing, who will talk 'pro union' in the locker room, on the shop floor, when they're out for a beer, who will take on the union's work wherever they go." Those gathered at the convention had to recognize, DeConcini urged, that "you and I can't do this job alone. . . ."

In summarizing the accomplishments of the 1982 convention, the *BC&T News* presented what could have stood as a portrait of the organization for the 1980s. Expanded support for educational conferences would tighten the "muscle and guts" of the organization, reaching the second- and third-tier leaders, the shop stewards and local members involved in the daily struggle. A new position of Director of Organization would further stimulate the International's drive to reach the tens of thousands still unorganized in its jurisdiction. Increased authorization of voluntary contributions to BC̆T-PAC, raised to 50 cents per member per month, would deflect assaults against the workers' standard of living and "the attempts by the right wing and their corporate cronies to turn the neutral tools of government (like the NLRB) against unions."

172

In 1979, a year after John DeConcini became president of the International, he became a member of the AFL-CIO Executive Council. It was an appropriate recognition of a man and a Union whose experience reflected in microcosm the more general challenges of the labor movement of the 1980s. The political ambivalence he faced among bakers in the 1970s and 1980s was widespread in labor's legions and stimulated the AFL-CIO's vast efforts in political education and campaigning in 1984. The contrasts he agonized over—30,000 BC&T pensioners, for instance, enjoying a retirement secured by one of the largest and best union pension funds, while BC&T membership continued to slip, down 6,700 in the three years prior to 1984—were mirrored across the board in sister unions experiencing massive managerial and technological change.

Finally, DeConcini's overall philosophy seemed to draw out the best of the trade union tradition and distill it in a form most likely to see the movement through a difficult period of adjustment. In it could be found a determination to organize the unorganized; to deliver more effective representation on the shop floor and at the bargaining table; to carry forth effective political action not only on issues of immediate interest to his members in their shops but also on a broader political plane in league with other progressive movements among women, minorities, retired people, young people and other allies. Underlying it all was an intangible fervor that has been the hallmark of labor leadership in the hardest of times and at its best. In his own Union, DeConcini was reaching out to his members, 1,100 in 13 educational conferences in 1982 alone.

Whatever problems the BC&T was to face, it would be hard to bet against a man who understood that the most important thing to tell a 1983 graduating class at the George Meany Center for Labor Studies was to "get out there on the stump and work as disciples, evangels and preachers to make sure the American people know of the great contributions the trade union movement has made to this country."

A four week strike in November and December 1972 involved 12,000 BC&T members, primarily at ITT-Continental plants, who were seeking a five-consecutive-day work-week.

Appendix

Major National Leaders of the Bakery, Confectionery and Tobacco Workers International Union, and its Predecessors

1. Officers of the Journeymen Bakers' National Union:
   George Block, Secretary, 1886-88
   August Delebar, Secretary, 1888-1890

2. Officers of the Journeymen Bakers' and Confectioners' International Union:
   August Delebar, Secretary, 1890-92
   George Horn, Secretary, 1892-95
   Henry Weismann, Secretary, 1895-97
   John Schudel, Secretary, 1897-99
   Frank Harzbecker, Secretary, 1899-1903

3. Officers of the Bakery and Confectionery Workers International Union:
   ʼFrank Harzbecker, Secretary, 1903-07
   Otto Fischer, Secretary, 1908-12; Financial Secretary, 1912-15
   Andrew Myrup, Treasurer, 1908-23; Secretary-Treasurer, 1923-41; President, 1941-43
   Charles Hohmann, Editor, 1908-23; Corresponding and Recording Secretary, 1923-36; Financial Secretary, 1936
   Charles Iffland, Corresponding and Recording Secretary, 1912-23
   Henry Koch, Financial Secretary, 1915-36
   Joseph Schmidt, Corresponding and Recording Secretary, 1936-41; Second Vice-President, 1941-43
   Herman Winter, Financial Secretary, 1936-41, First Vice-President, 1941-43; President, 1943-1950
   William Schnitzler, Second Vice-President, 1943-46; Secretary-Treasurer, 1946-50; President, 1950-52
   James Cross, Secretary-Treasurer, 1950-52; President, 1952-57

4. Officers during the Split:
   A. Bakery and Confectionery Workers International Union:
      James Cross, President, 1957-61
      James Landriscina, President, 1961-62
      Max Kralstein, President, 1962-69

   B. American Bakery and Confectionery Workers International Union:
      Dan Conway, President, 1957-69
      Curtis Sims, Assistant to the President for Financial Affairs, 1957-58; Secretary-Treasurer, 1958-1969
      John DeConcini, Executive Vice-President, 1957-69; Secretary-Treasurer, 1969

5. Officers of the Bakery and Confectionery Workers International Union from the Merger:
   Dan Conway, President, 1969-78
   Max Kralstein, Secretary-Treasurer, 1969-70
   Greg Oskoian, Executive Vice-President, 1969-70, Secretary-Treasurer, 1970-78
   John DeConcini, Executive Vice-President, 1969-1978, President, 1978
   Joseph Kane, Executive Vice-President, 1969-1978
   Earl Tetrick, Executive Vice-President, 1969-1978

6. Officers of the Bakery, Confectionery and Tobacco Workers International Union:
   John DeConcini, President, 1978-present
   Greg Oskoian, Secretary-Treasurer, 1978
   René Rondou, Executive Vice-President, 1978, Secretary-Treasurer, 1978-present
   Joseph Kane, Executive Vice-President, 1978-79
   Earl Tetrick, Executive Vice-President, 1978-present

Index

Adams, Enoch George, 1
Alvino, Henry, 100, 110-11, 117, 138-39, 154-55, 160
Almagamated Food Workers, 72, 93, 114
American Bakery and Confectionery Workers International Union, 147-165; affiliates with the AFL-CIO, 148; launches Union and Industry Welfare Fund and Pension Fund, 149-50; begins publishing *ABC News,* 149
American Bakeries, 100
American Baking Company, 63, 65, 75, 90
American Bisquit Company, 51-52
American Federation of Labor, 6, 13, 20, 25, 52, 80, 89, 96-97, 105-06, 115-16, 132, 137
American Federation of Labor—Congress of Industrial Organizations, 142-44, 149-51, 153-56, 168, 170, 173
American Press Bureau, 86
American Stores Bakeries, 109
Anderson, Hjalmer, 112
Apollo Candy Company, 95
Associated Industries, 86
Atlantic & Pacific Tea Company, 75, 90-93, 100, 113, 128, 150, 152, 166
Audette, Arthur J., 36
Aumiller, Charles, 166
Bacon, Martin, 137
Bakers' and Confectioners' Alliance, 35
Bakery and Confectionery Workers International Union, Socialism in, 1, 3,

18, 24-29, 35-36, 54, 57, 70, 105-06; founded as Journeymen Bakers National Union of the United States, 5-7; chooses New York City for first headquarters, 7; establishes journal, 7, 16, 41; affiliates with AFL, 13; relations with the Knights of Labor, 13-21; in Canada, 17, 51, 64, 77-79, 86, 100, 102, 135-36; adopts the name Journeymen Bakers' and Confectioners' International Union, 23; political action in, 25-28, 35, 38-39, 54-55, 57, 105, 163, 170-73; moves Executive Board to Cleveland, 26; moves Executive Board to Chicago, 26; strike fund, 26, 28-29, 42, 55-56, 58, 60, 74, 92; sick and death benefit, 26, 31, 38, 41, 43, 54, 58, 60, 135; retirement benefits, 28, 91; unemployment benefits, 28, 40, 43, 54, 56, 58, 98-100, 102-03; business unionism in, 28-29, 38-42, 54-58, 74, 92, 105; moves headquarters to Brooklyn, 31; local autonomy in, 41-43, 54, 57, 71, 87, 90, 92, 130, 132, 152; moves headquarters to Cleveland, 42; use of label, 49-50, 52, 55-56, 70, 73, 75-76, 87, 92, 96, 100-01, 118; women in, 51, 53, 55, 79, 95, 107, 110-14, 120, 171; adopts name Bakery and Confectionery Workers International Union, 53; organizing system, 53-54, 56, 74, 92, 119, 135-36, 172; moves headquarters to Chicago, 56; auxiliaries, 56, 70-72, 83, 95, 111; worksharing in, 62, 98-99,

177

102; blacks in, 75, 82-83, 127, 129, 166-68; in the South, 82-83, 85, 106-07, 110, 127-29, 140, 166-68; purchase of headquarters building in Chicago, 91; confectionery workers in, 94-96, 106-07, 110, 113-18, 136, 152, 165-69; cracker workers in, 95, 106-07, 114-17, 127, 152; ice cream workers in, 96; pretzel workers in, 106, 111; macaroni and noodle workers in, 106, 165; industrial unionism in, 53, 111-12, 116; adopts presidential system, 119; joint negotiations, 126-31, 134-35, 149-50, 166-68; national welfare fund, 131, 135, 148-50; pension fund, 131, 135, 148-50; moves headquarters to Washington, D.C., 137-38; Committee to Preserve Integrity, 140, 142-43, 145, 147; reunification committee, 154; Local Unions Reunification Committee, 154-55, 160; buys Solar Building, 157; merges with ABC, 161

Bakery and Confectionery Workers International Union, ethnic groups, Austrian, 24, 38, 41; Bohemian, 10, 30, 34, 46; Dutch, 45; French, 46; German, 1, 4-6, 9-11, 13-16, 18, 20, 24-25, 30, 32, 34, 40-41, 46-47, 49, 79-80, 82, 93, 108, 110-11, 125, 166; Hispanic, 112, 127; Irish, 3-5, 16, 32, 82, 95; Italian, 45-46, 82, 95, 115; Jewish, 24, 45-46, 61-62, 82, 93, 95, 98, 136; Polish, 82, 94; Scandinavian, 30, 46, 51, 112-13; Swiss, 24, 40; Syrian, 95

Bakery and Confectionery Workers International Union, local activity, Albany, New York, 18, 32; Allentown, Pennsylvania, 111; Amarillo, Texas, 94; Aurora, Illinois, 87; Baltimore, Maryland, 7, 13-14, 23, 82, 89, 93, 98-99; Birmingham, Alabama, 82; Boston, Massachusetts, 7, 13, 17, 21, 29, 31, 35, 42, 51, 61, 66, 70, 82, 89, 93, 95; Brantford, Canada, 79; Bridgeport, Connecticut, 7, 29; Brockton, Massachusetts, 35, 51; Brooklyn, New York, 1, 6-9, 12, 14-15, 18, 20, 23, 32, 40, 62, 65-66, 72-73, 82, 89, 114; Buffalo, New York, 6-7, 32, 50, 57, 66, 73-74, 90, 93, 98-100; Charleston, South Carolina, 129; Chat-

tanooga, Tennessee, 100, 110, 127; Chicago, Illinois, 3, 6-7, 24, 30-31, 35, 49-53, 57, 63, 66, 70, 74-75, 78, 83, 86-90, 95-97, 101, 112-13, 117, 140, 149, 152, 155; Cincinnati, Ohio, 6, 9, 23, 47, 63, 74, 111, 151; Cleveland, Ohio, 7, 18, 24, 26, 42, 66-67, 89-90, 94, 113-14, 143, 151; Columbus, Ohio, 151; Dallas, Texas, 85, 94; Dayton, Ohio, 74; Denver, Colorado, 49-50, 62-63, 93-94, 100; Detroit, Michigan, 6-7, 12, 30, 93-94, 117, 142; Edmonton, Canada, 77; Elizabeth, New Jersey, 12; Fall River, Massachusetts, 76; Fargo, North Dakota, 85; Fort worth, Texas, 94; Hamilton, Canada, 77; Hamilton, Ohio, 100, 136; Hartford, Connecticut, 7; Haverhill, Massachusetts, 76; Hershey, Pennsylvania, 117-18; Hoboken, New Jersey, 65; Hot Springs, Arkansas, 100; Indianapolis, Indiana, 6-7, 13, 26; Jacksonville, Florida, 166; Jersey City, New Jersey, 12, 18; Joplin, Missouri, 152; Kansas City, Missouri, 7, 109, 126, 150, 152, 167; Lawrence, Kansas, 76; Lincoln, Nebraska, 167-68; Little Rock, Arkansas, 100; London, Canada, 77, 79; Los Angeles, California, 68, 86, 93, 116, 140, 154, 160; Louisville, Kentucky, 7; Lowell, Massachusetts, 76; Marion, South Carolina, 168; Medicine Hat, Canada, 77; Milwaukee, Wisconsin, 6-7, 10-11, 13, 23, 45, 94, 103, 150; Minneapolis, Minnesota, 23, 45, 93, 152; Montreal, Canada, 77, 136; Montrose, Colorado, 167; Moose Jaw, Canada, 77; New Bradford, Massachusetts, 76; New Haven, Connecticut, 6, 85; New Orleans, Louisiana, 6-7, 23, 63, 66, 80, 83, 110; New York, New York, 1-10, 12, 15, 18, 20, 23, 27, 29-37, 40, 42, 45-47, 50-52, 57, 60-62, 65-66, 70-74, 89, 93, 95, 99, 111-12, 114-15, 126, 139, 152, 154-56, 158; Newark, New Jersey, 3, 6-7, 12, 18, 23, 29, 35, 51, 75, 77-78, 87, 89, 96, 122, 158; Oakland, California, 152; Omaha, Nebraska, 7; Ottawa, Canada, 79; Passaic, New Jersey, 158; Paterson, New Jersey, 47, 80, 158; Pe-

178

Roosevelt, Franklin, 106, 109
Roseman's Bakery, 108
Ross, Herman, 67, 75
Rowe, James, 143
Russell Stover, 167-68
Safeway Grocery and Baking Company, 150
Saniel, Lucien, 27
Schad, Herman, 110
Schirra, Rudolf, 82
Schlemmer, Leo, 24
Schmidt, John, 21
Schmidt, Joseph, 38, 54, 90, 94, 102, 105-06, 108, 119-23
Schneider, Frank, 81
Schneider, R. C., 81
Schnitzler, William, 96, 121-23, 127, 129-33, 136-37, 147, 151, 160
Schudel, John, 3, 6-7, 12, 23, 28, 30, 34, 38-46, 54, 57
Schulze Baking Company, 87
Schumacher, William, 130
Searry, A. B., 129
Segal, Martin & Company, 148
Seidel, August, 10-11
Shields, Charles D., 68
Shults Bread Company, 65-66, 73, 90, 126
Siebold, George, 155
Simmons, A. M., 56
Simmons, John, 130
Sims, Curtis, 100, 110, 127-29, 135, 138-44, 146-48, 152, 159-61
Socialist Labor Party, 18, 25, 27 29, 35-36
Socialist Trade and Labor Alliance, 35
Spang Bakery, 113
Speck Bakery, 113
Stack, Edward, 124
Star Bakery, 113
Stuart, George, 130, 134, 137, 139-42, 144, 155
Suffrin, A., 136
Sullivan, Peter, 155
Sunshine Bisquit, 139
Taft-Hartley Act, 130, 137
Tastee Cake Baking Company, 109
Teamsters, Chauffeurs, Warehousemen, and Helpers of America, International Union of, 75, 96-97, 100, 113, 117, 140, 142, 145, 153-54, 156, 159-60
Tetrick, Earl, 152, 159
Thatcher, Herbert, 131

Thompson, Hope, 88
Tobacco Workers International Union, 169
Tobin, Daniel, 75, 97
Triplett, Gean, 154
Tulley, Austin, 152
Turner, Fred, 13
United Bakeries Corporation, 90
United Hebrew Trades, 62, 73
United States Bisuit Company, 51
Vicars, A. W., 17, 19
Waldo, F. J., 37
Walker, B. H., 106
Walsh, James, 23
Walsh, Joseph, 78-79, 82
War Labor Board, 122
Ward, Louis L., 168
Ward, William B., 66, 89-90, 97
Ward Baking Company, 66-69, 72, 74, 77-78, 81-82, 87-91
Ward Baking Corporation, 92, 100, 111, 113, 116, 130
Ward-Mackey Baking Company, 67
Ward Motor Vehicle Company, 66
Weber, John, 79
Wehofer, Sam, 110, 130
Weismann, Henry L., 27, 29, 31, 35, 40, 41, 43
White, Earl, 111
Whitman's Candy Company, 110
Wille, Marcel, 68, 82
Williams, Edward Bennett, 139
Wilson, S. D., 116
Winter, Herman, 81, 108-09, 119-21, 125-27, 129, 134, 138, 142
Wise, Stephen, 62
Wismer, Alma, 95
Women's Trade Union League, 62, 95
World War I, 76-83, 95, 113, 136
World War II, 120, 122, 126
Zamford, Jack, 45, 75, 92-93, 102, 106, 120
Zion Industries, Incorporated, 140